Five Years In A Persian Town

by

Napier Malcolm

Five Years
In A Persian Town
by Napier Malcolm

ISBN: 978-93-61424-55-7

Published by

DOUBLE 9 BOOKS

2/13-B, Ansari Road
Daryaganj, New Delhi – 110002
info@double9books.com
www.double9books.com
Tel. 011-40042856

ABOUT THE AUTHOR

Napier Malcolm was a pioneering British anthropologist and writer recognized for his groundbreaking paintings in the subject of ethnography. His masterpiece, "Five Years in a Persian Town," stands as a testomony to his keen observational competencies and deep information of Persian way of life. In this seminal work, Malcolm offers readers with a brilliant and insightful portrait of lifestyles in a small town in Persia (cutting-edge-day Iran) in the course of the early twentieth century. Drawing upon his stories living among the nearby populace for five years, Malcolm gives a richly targeted account of the social customs, spiritual practices, and each day exercises of the townspeople. Through meticulous research and attractive prose, Malcolm explores a wide variety of subjects, including family lifestyles, education, exchange, and governance, dropping mild on the intricacies of Persian society and its traditions. He additionally delves into the demanding situations and opportunities dealing with the city inside the midst of political and social exchange, presenting readers a nuanced knowledge of the forces shaping life in the vicinity. "Five Years in a Persian Town" isn't always best a fascinating ethnographic take a look at but also a compelling narrative that immerses readers within the sights, sounds, and reports of a bygone technology.

CONTENTS

PREFACE 7

CHAPTER I..9

CHAPTER II 25

CHAPTER III..35

CHAPTER IV...58

CHAPTER V 68

CHAPTER VI...90

CHAPTER VII..102

CONCLUSION..120

FOOTNOTES..123

GLOSSARY 124

INDEX 127

PREFACE

I feel that this short sketch of a Persian town needs an apology. It will not improbably be mistaken for a book of travel. Stopping five years in one place is not travelling, and the experience of such a stay is not a traveller's experience. The descriptions that will be found in this volume refer to a very small area, and consequently a good deal of minute work has been attempted that would have been out of place in the painting of a larger sphere.

Then, again, this is not a book upon mission work. There is comparatively little about the very interesting work which is being carried on in Yezd by the Church Missionary Society, but there is a great deal about the circumstances under which missionaries work, for the book is really a description of a Persian town from the missionary point of view. This will explain why certain details, such as the dress and food of the people, are left out altogether; for, although there may be some connection between these things and the kind of way in which missionary work ought to be conducted, it is not at present apparent to the writer. On the other hand, the general effects of house, street, and desert, which meet the Yezdi's eye at every turn, have been rather elaborately described, for scenery and scenic surroundings have much effect on character, and the study of character is essential in missionary work.

In most of the descriptions I have taken special care to preserve the true proportion between good and evil, so far as I have been able to estimate it in the thing described. I have specially done this in the necessarily incomplete sketches which I have drawn of the Yezdi's character and religious beliefs. But in dealing with the Persian Government I have consciously deviated from this practice. Consequently, I must ask the reader to regard all references to the Government as going no further than the actual statements. I have also, as far as possible, avoided alluding to political problems; for, in a country like Persia, for a man engaged in serious missionary work abstention from politics is almost a *sine qua non*.

It will, perhaps, be felt by some that more ought to be made of the points in common between Islam and Christianity. The fact is that when people come to the missionary they do not want to find agreement but disagreement, and consequently the missionary gets to think not so much of what they know as of what they do not know. So a missionary writer is, perhaps, inclined to pass over common points, whatever religion he is writing about. In the case of Islam there are really not many to note, and in support of this statement I may relate a story told by an officer of Indian troops. One day a Mohammedan, in the course of a conversation, said to him: "Of course, Sahib, your religion and ours are very near together. Your Christ is one of our prophets." My friend replied: "What do you mean? Of course Christ is one of your prophets, but to us He is more than a prophet; He is the Son of God and the pattern of our lives. Besides there is hardly a single practical point where Mohammedans and Christians are not entirely at issue." The man looked up and said: "Sahib, you have read the Quran, and you have read your Bible. I always make that remark to Christians: I made it to a padre the other day: and they almost always say, 'Very true; Mohammedanism has a great deal in common with Christianity.' Well, Sahib, when they say that, I know that they have not read the Quran and they have not read their Bibles."

My best thanks are due to Miss Mary Bird, whose name is well known both in Persia and to all interested in that country, for the valuable assistance that she has given me out of the wide and unique experience that she possesses on the subjects handled in my book. I am also very grateful to the Rev. G. Furness Smith for several valuable suggestions.

I am indebted to the Rev. C. H. Stileman and to Mr Paul Peter for some of the photographs illustrating the book. The coloured prints and the picture of the School are from drawings by a native artist, Mirza Abu'l Qasim.

CHAPTER I

In the very centre of central Persia there is a town called Yezd, which in some ways may be uninteresting, but ought for a student of Persia to have the greatest interest, for it possesses all the regular attributes of a Persian town to an exaggerated degree. These Persian towns can be better understood after some consideration of the country in which they lie. Some one, I think, has said that Persia consists of two parts, the salt desert, and the desert which is not salt; and though this is not true of all parts of Persia, with regard to most of the interior of Persia it is as nearly true as a reasonable man can expect an aphorism to be. In the vast district where Yezd lies you find an archipelago, with sand for sea, and towns and villages for islands. If you want to know how big that desert area is, I can only tell you that we went to Yezd, which lies in the very centre of Persia, from the southern shore of the Caspian, which is the northern boundary of the country, and with the exception of a belt of land at the extreme north about thirty miles broad, and a patch round Teheran about twenty miles across, we literally passed through nothing but desert.

But desert in Persia is of many kinds: even the salt desert is not all the same. There are places where the ground is absolutely bare, except for the thick crusts of salt that lie like snowdrifts streaking the surface in every direction. There are also places equally salt where the proximity of a certain amount of useless water produces a larger quantity of plant life than in most parts of the ordinary desert. The ordinary desert is good soil, and wherever water can be brought to it, it is extremely fertile. Generally it has a hard but rather gravelly surface. Sometimes it is flecked with dry brownish shrubs about the size of bedding-out plants, sometimes it is quite bare. There is in parts a good deal of scattered growth, but two plants never touch one another. In the more favourable places shrubs may be found at an average of not more than two yards apart, but, with one exception, I have never seen in the desert plains of central Persia a place away from the hills with sufficient natural growth to modify the colour of the distance.

Then there is the sandy desert. Here also, if the sand is scraped away and water brought, the soil is good, but in appearance the sandy desert is the most desolate of all. Absolutely nothing grows on it. It is like the worst kind of salt desert, without the relief of the white patches. Yezd lies in a big stretch of sandy desert. Sometimes the sand may be broken by a large piece of gravelly plain, but such places are generally as bare as the sands themselves, and form no real break in the dull monotony.

Of course there are oases; but what is called an oasis is not really very different in character from the desert that surrounds it. It is the same desert artificially cultivated. In the plains the water is brought from a distance, and when it is applied the ground consents to nourish exactly those seeds that have been sown. There are hardly any weeds, no turf, no tangle, no hedges, and no waste green. Every blade in the artificial wheat-field is an isolated unit, that may be pulled up without disturbing its neighbour. Even in the fresher-looking gardens, enclosed and concealed by high mud walls, there is the same meagre, bedded-out appearance on every side. In spite of the possibility of three artificial harvests in the year, one sees at a glance that the very roots will inevitably be annihilated when the water is cut off, and of course this happens pretty frequently. There are no wild trees at all, and those that are reared are very small, and scanty in leafage. Such oases as these go by different names, according to the quantity of water. Those that can support a fairly large population are towns, those that can support a smaller one are villages, those that can only support one or two households are called cultivations, or *mazra's*. But, however big or however small, they are no interruption to the continuity of the desert.

In the hills and round their bases there is a trifle more plant life, but there is no strong contrast to the barrenness below. Only high up in the creases of the mountain sides, right above the cultivations and villages, there are the narrowest strips of turf on either side of the snow torrents. Here one may find small ferns nestling under the boulders, and quantities of soft flowers, or an occasional wild barberry bush. Away from the actual bed of the mountain streams one is again in desert of a kind, though here, too, the scattered dry shrubs will be found alternating with more succulent varieties of plants, and the landscape is by no means entirely bare.

As soon as these streams reach ground that it is possible to level into terraces, they are used for irrigation, and become the stalks of minute *mazra's*. Then come long hill villages with orchard trees and walnuts; and lastly, if there is any water left at the real mountain base, there will be a round irrigated patch of rather larger extent on the edge of the plain.

In the middle of the plains water may be found about sixty yards beneath the surface, a depth from which it may be drawn through wells for drinking purposes, but not in large quantities for irrigation. Consequently, if the snow torrents were the only source of water supply, the centres of the Persian plains would be uninhabitable; for in districts like that of Yezd the rainfall is so trifling that nine or ten not over large falls of rain or snow in the twelve months constitute a wet year. But water that is found at sixty, or even a hundred, yards down at the base of the hills is by no means useless. From this point to the centre of the plain there is a considerable, though very gradual declivity. So when the original shaft has been sunk, and water has been found, perhaps at three hundred feet below the surface, a long line of similar shafts are sunk towards the centre of the desert, at distances varying from twenty to forty yards, the line sometimes stretching for more than thirty miles, until a point of desert has been reached that lies as deep down as the original water-level. Then all the shafts are connected at the bottom by burrows, just big enough to afford passage to a man; the water is let in, and appears in an open ditch in the centre of the desert. Of course conveyance of water by these *qan'āts* as they are called, which are often thirty or forty miles long, is by no means inexpensive, so as a rule the water is used immediately it can be brought to the surface. Consequently we find all through the barren Persian plains two strange phenomena: little cultivations, fed by artificial channels, standing all by themselves, leagues away from anywhere, in the middle of a desolate and waterless expanse; and large towns such as Yezd, situated far away from any natural water supply, in the barest spot to be found in all the desert, the central hollow where the drifting sands have collected and covered over even the faintest vestige of vegetable life.

HUJJATABAD, THE FIRST STAGE FROM YEZD.
Sandy desert, with qan'at pits in foreground.

The typical Persian plain is very long, appearing to be comparatively narrow, and certainly flat beyond conception. The plains through which one approaches Yezd from Kashan or Kirman are probably on the average about sixty miles broad. But the huge barren mountains, lying in long jagged ranges to the right and left, show with such plainness of detail from every point, that the traveller unused to the clear atmosphere of the East can hardly credit the full size and distance. Mountains, plains, foreground, and far perspective, everything, in the Yezd district at any rate, is one neutral tint of brown, except for the snow lying on the rocks of the mountain-top, the long flakes of salt scattered here and there about the plain, or the continual moving mirage. Even at sunrise and sunset, when the sky and distant hills put on a colouring of glorious brilliancy, there is an utter absence of those soft tones in the foreground which can only be given by sunlight in a humid atmosphere.

Near Yezd there rise into sight brown villages, excrescences of the same material as that on which they stand, isolated separate objects with sharp definite bounds. The scanty, hedgeless crops that surround them, usually arranged in oblong patches like small allotments, seldom show until the traveller is quite near; the few trees are wretchedly poor in size and colour, and the walls and buildings are simply mud, of which three parts are in ruins.

After a few of these villages we come to Yezd itself, equally isolated from everything, and in other respects very much the same as the villages. However, as we approach the town by most of the main roads, there are no fields and no trees at all. Also there are sticking out from the town a lot of high square air-shafts, looking like short factory chimneys. Yezd, like the villages, is brown, but there are a few patches of white. There are one or two very faintly tiled minarets and a newer-looking green dome; but these things are not sufficiently striking to modify the general brown effect.

Now we are among the *bāghs*.[1] A *bāgh* is an enclosure, generally oblong, consisting of mud walls twelve feet high, surrounding a planted area. Very often a *bagh* contains nothing but fields of farm crops. The better class *baghs*, belonging to the richer Persians, have in the centre a kind of summer dwelling-house with plenty of porticos, built on a very open-air pattern. Such *baghs* are well stocked with fruit trees and rose bushes; there may also be a few small elms, or short poplars, or perhaps some cypresses. There are not many flowers. Here, too, most of the area is given up to farm crops. Everything is laid out after the plan of a Dutch garden, but without the turf and thick foliage, and also without the extreme trimness that we connect with such places. In the better gardens there is always a small gutter of running water, and generally an artificial tank with a stone border. This is the part of the *bagh* most highly prized by the natives. In Persia a small artificial channel with a stream of water about two feet across seems to give that air of distinction to a house which we expect from a well-kept lawn with good flower-beds. From the road nothing can be seen of all this greenery except the tops of the highest trees. In Yezd indeed only the *baghs* that lie some way out up the course of the *qan'ats* show as much as this. Just round the town nothing is to be seen but the bare walls and the gateways of the gardens. The gateways have some brickwork about them, and are sometimes partially whitened. They stand back from the road. The tops of the mud walls are generally in bad repair, and here and there we come across a jagged hole that has been made as a short cut into the garden by the gardener. In such cases the pieces of mud and sun-dried bricks, when they have been taken out, lie in the street. Where the surface of the thoroughfare has not been taken up for bricks, which by the way are left to bake in the sun in the middle of the road, it is generally used for drying manure that has been kneaded with a modicum of earth. The dyers also use the street for hanging up their cloths to dry, and also for arranging their skeins of silk, which they twist round wooden pegs stuck into the wall about forty yards apart. The road surface is a little irregular, and occasionally it is made more interesting by a shaft leading into a *qan'at*. As we approach the houses proper the road narrows, for it is only the natural lane between enclosures, and the house enclosures, which from the outside are exactly similar to the *baghs*, lie closer together.

Occasionally, as we near the centre of the town, we come across open squares with a small mosque on the one side. The wall of the mosque is dirty white, and there is a little black lettering over the doorway, but very little tile or brick. In the middle there may be a dilapidated octagon with a flat top, about five feet high and six across, built of mud covered with tiles rather the worse for wear. Round such squares there are generally arched recesses, filled in at the bottom, so as to make a ledge three feet from the ground. The bazaars are just the old narrow lanes, covered by a succession of mud domes forming a continuous but untidy roof. The goods are displayed on tiers of mud ledges, and there is a mud room behind. Quantities of the wares are mud. Firepans, barrels for grain, several kinds of toys, bread receptacles, and some other household implements are simply clay, moulded into a rough form, and dried in the sun. Water-bottles, various kinds of pitchers, children's money-boxes, and hookah-bowls are baked with fire, but without the slightest glaze. The baker's ovens are made of mud, down to the very doors. Many of the Yezdis even eat mud, and develop an unwholesome muddy complexion.

The cleverness of the Yezdi in manipulating mud is beyond belief. Sometimes you may see men in the streets making barrels for storing grain. First of all a smooth round slab of mud about an inch and a half thick, is moulded on the ground. Then another piece of mud is kneaded into a long sausage, and placed in a hoop upon the edge of the slab. Sausage after sausage is added hoopwise, one on the top of the other, until a height of about four feet has been reached. Each hoop, as it is laid in position, is worked with the hand into smooth connection with the hoop below, and when the barrel is completed there is not the least vestige of a join. The whole is done without wheel or machinery of any kind. A mud lid is added which is soldered on with mud when the barrel is filled.

I have hardly yet succeeded in giving any adequate impression of the untidiness of the streets. The central courtyard of the house is generally a fair-sized garden. For reasons connected with the water supply the inhabitants of the houses are continually altering the level of these places, and large quantities of earth are emptied into the street or carried out of it every day as occasion may arise. All along the sides of the streets there are shallow holes for rubbish heaps; here and there there are cesspools; and yet with all this the streets are so well scavenged by dogs and children that, except in the Jewish quarter, the thoroughfare is comparatively clean, while, thanks to the powerful sun and the absolute absence of moisture in the atmosphere, almost the only obtrusive smells from one end of the town to the other are those that hang round the public baths and the places used by the dyers.

Let us now enter one of the doorways that leads into a better class house. We find ourselves first of all in a round or octagonal porch, covered by a small dome, which is generally pierced in the centre to admit light. From this porch we go through a passage into one of the court-yards. In a good house there are two, or even three court-yards. The whole family live in the better compound, and the men receive their visitors in the smaller one. Though this rule is not without exception, the better class women in Yezd do not seem to have much to complain of in the matter of housing.

In the court-yard there will be found an open tank and some flower-beds; the rest is generally paved. The flower-beds are below the level of the pavement, and are irrigated from the tank. Watering-pots are used for watering the pavement only. Sometimes the whole garden is sunk to the level of the cellar floor, so as to get nearer to the *qan'at*. The house itself consists of two sets of buildings, chiefly one story, with perhaps one or two upstairs rooms. The upper rooms, however, do not really form a separate story, but are built over the lowest of the ground-floor rooms, so as to bring the roof more or less to one level. The roofs are generally paved with flat bricks of the shape of tiles, and are surrounded by a low mud wall, so as to form a more or less secluded and cool place, where the family may sleep in summer. Perhaps a dome may partially project above the level of the rest of the roof. Also there is the inevitable *bād-gīr*, or square air-shaft, running down to the back of the big summer portico, or *tālār*, and furnished at the top with long slits on all four sides to catch any air that may be moving. This *talar* is the principal room on the summer side, which faces north. It is often built in the form of a cross with very stumpy arms, or rather of an oblong with the corners so taken off as to render it slightly cruciform. The long side of the oblong faces the court-yard, and has no wall at all, but there is a curtain of tent-cloth that moves up and down on pulleys. To the right and left of this sun-blind are short walled-off passages, which are used as entrances. Corresponding to the projecting front part between the passages there is at the back a recess under the *bad-gir*, completing the cruciform design. The roof is arched into a high dome. The whole *talar* is raised three feet above the level of the garden, so as to give room for a two-foot upright grating, which is the window of the cellar room underneath. For five months in the year these are the only habitable rooms in a Persian house; and they are both furnished as living-rooms. The rooms on either side of the *talar* are so like the winter rooms that it is unnecessary to describe them separately.

The whole structure of the place is quite different from that of an English building. Except for enclosing a rough garden the Persian builder hardly ever makes a blank wall. Sometimes the walls of the compound, generally the walls of stables and outhouses, but always the sides of rooms, passages, and porticos consist of a series of arches more or less carefully moulded. In the house, unless they are intended for doors, windows, or cupboards, these arched recesses are filled in to a height of three feet; so that round every Persian room there is a series of ledges, called *tāqchas*, about the size of a small mantelpiece, generally a span deep, but sometimes very much deeper, and running in instead of running out. If the height of the room will allow it, there is a line of straight moulding above these arches, and above that a second row, usually much shorter than the lower ones. Above that comes a second series of lines of straight moulding, shelving into the arch of the roof, for the ceilings are always constructed on the arch principle, although they are sometimes flattened on the top when it is intended to build an upper room. These arches are built of brick and mud only, without any wood or wooden foundation; and indeed no wood is used in a Yezd house at all, except for doors and windows.

You will find three styles of wall in Persian houses. Sometimes the rough mud is coated over with a smoother surface, either clay and chopped straw, or clay and sand, and the brown colour is left unchanged. In fairly good houses this style is often thought good enough for the summer portico.

Very often the angles of the mouldings are pointed with white gypsum, and when ornamental designs in the same fashion are added, the effect is exceedingly pretty. But generally the living rooms in a Persian house are entirely whitened with gypsum, and a moulded design, about an eighth of an inch thick, is made in the centre of the ceiling. These complicated and accurate geometrical designs are produced by the natives with no better tools than a chisel and a bit of string. The formation of the arches and straight mouldings without instruments is equally wonderful, but though the appearance is geometrical two arches never exactly correspond with one another if one comes to measure. Still the construction of a Persian room, perhaps with a large dome, without any better materials than clay, gypsum, and a small modicum of baked brick, without any scaffolding or wooden basis, and with the help of none but the very simplest tools, is a thing that may be accounted one of the most extraordinary marvels of the East.

As in the summer, so in the winter side, the best room is generally in the centre. The better rooms are almost invariably approached from the side and not from the front, being separated from one another by passages that run to the whole depth of the buildings. This enables the entire frontage of the room to be given up to windows. Generally some of the rooms have a large cupboard room at the back, which is frequently used for sleeping in. As the floor of the house is three feet above the level of the compound, the passages between the rooms are furnished with steps, but they have no doors. Consequently, to shift one's quarters in such a house necessitates going into the open air. The smaller rooms are generally approached from the front, and in this case they sometimes have an *aivān*, or mud verandah. The winter rooms always take up the north end of the compound, but are often built along the east or west side as well.

Rooms are generally named by the number of their windows, which is usually three or five. A good five-windowed room will have a frontage of five arches filled in with French windows. The semi-circular fanlight consists of pieces of coloured glass fixed together in a wooden lattice. The lattice at a distance resembles fret-work, but is really elaborately pieced together. Some of the older windows contain exceedingly fine work, but even when it is well done it is not very durable, and nowadays they can only do very rough work. Some of the work that is forty or fifty years old is marvellous, but could not be done at the present time for love or money. The French window itself consists of two doors which are supposed to meet in the middle. There are no hinges, but each door has a wooden foot which turns in a mud socket. The arrangement of the coloured glasses which forms the panes is extremely artistic. The same sort of wooden lattice is used, but the pattern is rather larger than the pattern of the fanlight. As may be supposed, it is extremely difficult to keep these windows clean, for the panes, besides being very minute, are simply caught into grooves in the wood; and, as the work is done without any great accuracy, they very seldom fit. The doors are made after the same design as the windows, but they have wooden panels. They are often surmounted by a glazed fanlight. The wood of the doors and windows is covered with a yellowish-brown paint, and warps very badly, as it is used in an unseasoned state. Our cat could generally get in through a bolted door.

Of course there is no form of door fastening which can be used from both sides, and in this way as in others a Persian house is distinctly inconvenient. Still the style of building when fresh is very pretty. These masses of French windows with their coloured panes artistically arranged, the lines of white arches all along the sides, and the high-arched ceiling with its curious mouldings give the room an ecclesiastical appearance. At the back of the room there is not infrequently a corresponding line of door-windows, leading to one of those cupboard-rooms which I have before mentioned. This arrangement increases the regularity of the general design.

Before passing on to describe the furniture I must mention that there is one other totally different style of window, which lifts up in a sash, without pulleys, and is supported when open by metal stays. Also it is very common to find wooden lattices unglazed. Paper or calico is pasted over these in the winter.

There are one or two other forms of ornamentation that are not uncommon. Perhaps a line of painting, quaint but distinctly artistic, may run round the room just below the *taqchas*, giving the effect of a dado. Sometimes the roof is much more elaborately moulded, and is spangled with little bits of looking-glass; when this is not overdone the effect is pleasing. It is not uncommon to find very poor looking-glasses, about twelve by six inches, let into the walls. There are in almost every room rings attached to staples, which are intended to support the baby's hammock. Fireplaces are a European importation, but they are generally to be found in at least one room of the better class houses. They are almost always narrow, and comparatively high, so as to conform to the arch design, and they are made in the wall without any metal. The metal fittings of the room, such as hammock-rings, staples, and door and window latches, are made of whitened iron curiously engraved; and nails of the same material with very large heads, from one inch to three or four inches across, are used freely by the Persians for ornamenting woodwork.

The movable furniture of a Persian room is very simple. Curtains are not used very freely, and those that are used are rather scanty. Generally they are hung up by the corners without any string. In the men's apartments they are used more for doors than for windows. The favourite pattern is a very crude green or red with a large lozenge in the middle, like the design on a watered silk.

The only really valuable things in a Persian room are the carpets. In some cases these are laid right up to the walls, and a piece of drugget something less than a yard wide is also laid along the walls, usually on three sides of the room. In other cases there is a border of very thick clumsy felts arranged round the carpet which occupies the centre of the floor. The felts are self-coloured, with a small amount of stamped pattern. They have not got cut edges, but are made in one piece, consequently the shape is very inaccurate. They cost nearly as much as good carpets, and are often protected with druggets in the same way. In the place of honour, furthest from the door, is a mattress stuffed with cotton, covered with some sort of chintz or cretonne, and furnished with one or two very large round bolsters. In the winter there is also occasionally a *kursī* in evidence, but they are less common in Yezd than in other Persian towns. The *kursi* is a rough stool, about as high as a milking-stool, and about eighteen inches square, completely covered with cotton quilts and rugs, which trail on the ground on every side. Beneath this an iron brazier of lighted charcoal is placed, and the family tuck their legs underneath the wraps, and squat round the *kursi* on the floor. This, however, is not generally kept in the room except in the coldest weeks. During the remaining seasons the brazier is often brought in on a large copper tray, either for heating the room, or for keeping the teapot warm and for opium smoking. All copper and iron utensils in Persia, such as these trays and braziers, are carefully tinned.

Tables in Yezd are made in the roughest fashion, but the legs are nicely turned, the Yezd carpenters being greatly inferior to the turners, who are entirely distinct from them, and who produce very good work with the simplest class of hand-lathe worked with a bow. The carpenter, on the other hand, is incapable of putting up a shelf straight. He never dovetails, and he disguises the inaccuracy of his joints with plentiful deposits of clay.

Many of the Yezdis use little tables about three feet by two, and standing about twelve inches high. These are used only for tea-things. But tea is generally made by an inferior, standing at a tall table in the corner of the room. These tables are rather larger, not less than four feet by two. They stand as high as an English sideboard, and have a rough border of curved or dog-tooth pattern falling down from the slab, so that they very much suggest a rough dressing-table. They are often brought in and out of the rooms as they are wanted. People who wish to be thoroughly European in their manners sometimes have a larger table of the same kind permanently in the room, surrounded by a few bentwood chairs, which are brought up from Bombay, or folding-chairs with cane seats, which I think they bring from Isfahān, and about which the less said the better. Such a table is always covered by a white cloth, the most fashionable variety being a Turkey bath-towel.

These chairs and larger tables are no real part of Persian plenishing, while the tea-tables are being continually carried backwards and forwards, and are not necessary to the equipment of the room. Consequently the room does not present a very filled appearance. The few utensils which it contains, other than those mentioned, are placed upon the *taqchas*. On one of these *taqchas* may be seen a pair of *lālas*. The *lala* is a spring candlestick with a globe, and is, I believe, made in Europe. The candles are also imported. All lights in Persia have to be carefully protected from the wind, as the house is not a continuous building, but a series of outhouses. On another *taqcha* will be found a lamp, also of European manufacture. Persian lamps, which are simply saucers of native vegetable oil with a floating wick, are used freely about the house when a strong light is not required, but they have the disadvantage of blackening the gypsum of the walls. With regard to the imported lamps it is a curious thing that, although the lamps used are of the cheapest variety, with stems and reservoirs of blue or white glass, lamps with short stems, which might be brought into the country at an infinitely less cost, do not seem to have come into fashion. On a third *taqcha* is sure to be found a specimen of the Persian hookah, or *qaliān*. This is a most elaborate pipe, and is both made and bought in sections. The large bowls, however, when they are made of glass, are, I believe, imported; also some of the china heads.

Sometimes you will find on the *taqchas* a pair of European vases. In Yezd the pattern is almost always that of the hand rising up from a stand and grasping a tapered vessel. Sometimes also you will find cheap Continental oleographs, generally ladies' heads. These are bought by the pair, and you will find two copies of the same picture standing side by side. Another European import to which the Yezdis are much attached is a looking-glass. These are of the oblong shape, with varnished or gilt frames. Perhaps also one will see on the *taqchas* a covered glass vessel with a long spout, containing rose-water.

In the women's rooms there is occasionally a large wooden trunk for clothes, covered with gold and silver paper, and of a very clumsy design. The *taqchas* may be covered with plush cloths, and this is sometimes the case in the men's apartments. The women are also fond of highly ornamented trinket boxes.

SWEET EATING IN A *TALAR*.

This is the principal part of the summer buildings in a Persian house, and the bottom of the picture is the level of the compound. The room underneath is a living room, and is lighted by the grating under the *talar*. It is only used in the heat of the day. The door to the cellar staircase is seen on the right of the picture. The passage is the approach to the *talar* itself.

The three men are sitting in the ordinary Persian way round a tray of sweets. The Yezd sweets are remarkably good and have no coarse flavour. They eat them as we do cakes, but in rather larger quantities. This *talar* is a small one. The larger ones are generally cruciform in shape. It has no *bad-gir* (air-shaft) or front curtain.

The better class Yezd houses are exceedingly clean, and so on the whole are the people who live in them. In this Yezd is distinctly superior to some other Persian towns. The houses of the rather poorer classes in Yezd are dirtier, but they would compare favourably with those of a corresponding class in many parts of Europe. The very poor class are crowded together, many families to one house, and live in a condition of filth as great as the dry atmosphere will permit. You must remember that the native never removes his clothes for the night; indeed he only removes his clothes or washes his body when he goes to the public bath. The fee for admission is a mere trifle, but people do not go to the bath unless they have an absolutely clean set of clothes to change into when they have bathed. A few of the poor people take off their clothes on arriving at the bath and wash them, staying in the bath until they are dry enough to put on again. This, however, is exceptional, and generally speaking the difference in the standard of cleanliness accepted by the richer and poorer Yezdis is very large.

Houses that are not very new are always more or less tumble-down. The mud ceilings crack very easily, and the white gypsum flakes off at the slightest touch. The more essential parts of the structure are equally undurable. But you must remember that no Yezdi wants his house to last for ever. When the house is first of all built, a large chamber is made below the surface to receive the drainage, and the size of this is determined by the length of time the owner wishes his house to last, which is generally forty to fifty years. When the chamber is full, the rich occupants move to another house, and the house gradually falls to pieces. To the Yezdi an old house means a bad house, and this idea is so deeply rooted, that even in his *bagh* he seems to prefer young trees to those which have attained their full size. The idea of a residence which bears the marks of natural growth, and is not simply artificial, has never entered into the Yezdi's mind; and the absence of this to us familiar idea, has to be reckoned with in dealing with his character. Also it must be remembered that two-thirds of a Persian town, and three-quarters of a Persian village, is from various causes invariably in ruins. I suppose that in an English climate the best-built Yezd dwelling houses would remain standing for about a fortnight. In spite of their palatial design they are really nothing but mud huts, and when you live in them, or rather about them, for you are in the open air as often as you are inside, you learn their imperfections to your cost. Nobody can realise the immense amount of damage that can be done in a town like Yezd by a really wet day. Some while ago we had twenty-four hours of rain, which destroyed, I believe, about a couple of hundred roofs, and, what is worse, caused the older *qan'at* pits to fall in, blocking the water supply in some parts of the town for three months. Is there any other town in the world where a little extra rain causes a three months' drought? There is a story in Tehran about a Dutch Ambassador, who was so afraid of the roof falling down that in wet weather he invariably slept under the table. However he was a very tall man, and, when the catastrophe happened, he got his foot crushed.

Still the summer buildings in a Yezd house are really not bad. Generally speaking, the Persian builds well for heat and badly for cold. Yet the short Yezdi winter is a very severe one; and we, who are accustomed to a longer cold season, are astonished to see the philosophic way in which the Yezdi sets himself to endure the cold while it lasts, without taking any particular precautions to defend himself from it. The long window-front is a mass of spaces and cracks. Even when panes are not missing, daylight is frequently to be seen between the glass and the lattice, between the window and its frame, and sometimes between the frame and the wall. This of course is not including the crack between the two doors, which is often half an inch wide. Remember that every door in the house is a front door, leading into the open air, and you will get some idea of the provision made against the winter cold. The fact is that the Persian only understands two kinds of winter requirements, that of the hard living working-man who demands only the simplest shelter against the cold, and that of the man who on cold days can devote himself to keeping warm with a *kursi* in an inner apartment. A man who wants to do his work comfortably in any sort of weather is entirely beyond his calculation. On the few days when snow falls the merchants' offices are practically deserted, and no one but the smaller tradesmen and artisans goes to the bazaars.

The house, as I have said, is really built for a protection against heat. When I first went to Yezd I was surprised to find how tremendously the natives were affected by the hot weather. The native is certainly less affected than the European by the direct rays of the sun; but although something in the climate seems to tell on Europeans after two or three years' residence, I would back a fairly strong Englishman, furnished with a sun-helmet, against the average town Yezdi, to get through a piece of work on a hot day, or to keep up continuous hard work for a season or two. Consequently every Yezdi who can afford it tries to get away from town for at least two months of the year. The hill villages, which the Persians call *yailāq*, or summer quarters, lie about thirty miles away from the town. Every well-to-do Persian has a house in one or other of these villages, and there is a fashion about them, some being resorts chiefly patronised by the artisans, and some by the big merchants.

As most of the richer Persians have more than one house in the villages, Europeans generally have no great difficulty in hiring a place to stay at. The houses are left during the winter in charge of a villager, who uses the lower rooms only, the upper ones being then uninhabitable from the intense cold. Indeed the cold is so great that we were told that one winter the animals had been dying of thirst, as the water was frozen beyond the possibility of breaking the ice, and they had not fuel enough to melt it. The whole building is much rougher than the town house, though the roofs have to be made more carefully. The villages are very small and isolated, and the winter population is quite trifling. There is in these villages a little arable land, but the people depend chiefly on root-crops, nuts, and dried fruit for their winter stores, and on the produce of the sheep and goats. The animals are tended in summer by the children. The little boys spend most of their time up the walnut trees, throwing down leaves for them to eat, while the little ragged shepherdesses carry a twelve-foot staff for whacking the walnut trees, when they do not climb them in the same way as their brothers.

Those who go to the villages in the summer take with them everything they need in the way of carpets, furniture, and cooking utensils, also all groceries, and even wheat and charcoal; for the commonest things of this kind are often absolutely unprocurable. A rich Persian has stores frequently sent to him from Yezd during his stay. Even in Yezd some necessary store or other is almost always running short, so that something is generally at famine prices. This, of course, is due to the great isolation of the town. But in the villages it is intensified. Sometimes there will be no meat, at another time hardly any bread, and some years ago we found it almost impossible to procure milk, and were told by our Persian friends that they had the same difficulty. This eighteen-hour journey, with all the paraphernalia of the home, is the average Yezdi's only experience of foreign travel; and for this reason I have thought it necessary to give some account of what he sees and finds.

I have now done my best to describe in detail almost the whole of the Yezdi's surroundings, the furniture of his room, the pattern of his house, the streets of his town, and the vast deserts by which he is isolated from the world. When he gets up in the morning, he finds himself in a room practically containing nothing but a carpet, the walls and ceiling an expanse of white gypsum, and the *taqchas* provided with solitary objects upon which his eye can rest in turn without the slightest diversion to anything else. There is no confusion, but at the same time there is no arrangement. In such a room, with such furniture, the necessity for arrangement never occurs to him. He goes out into his court-yard; certainly there are flower-beds, but they are not cut like English flower-beds in the middle of necessarily existing growth and greenery. The shape of the beds and the nature of their contents has not been chosen with the slightest view to their artistic surroundings; they are simply artificial constructions in a waste of pavement which itself conceals the desert which stands to the Persian in the place of the natural world. Inside the beds each plant grows its own life, by itself, untouched by its neighbour, and the eye unconsciously fixes itself upon it as on an isolated unit. The Yezdi leaves his house and passes through an absolutely dry and scentless atmosphere along streets which present variety only in the matter of form. He goes for a journey across the desert plains; to the right there is only one object to be seen, a range of distant mountains, with a slight variety of jags along the top; to the left there is a similar range. Every now and again he comes across a shrub which attracts his eye by its hermit existence. Behind him is the solitary city; every six miles, while he is in the neighbourhood of the town, there is an equally solitary village, or perhaps a water-cistern with a domed roof; for league after league he can see in front of him his solitary *manzil*, where he intends to stay the night. Even when he goes to the villages this sparseness of life and circumstance is scarcely modified. Can you be surprised if this hourly contemplation of isolated units produces a mind which it is impossible for the tangle-reared European ever to fully understand? Can you be surprised if an intellect is produced accustomed to almost unbelievable concentration upon single and solitary ideas, but almost unreachable by minds that are accustomed to complicated trains of thought, to careful evasions of contradictions, and to systematic arrangements of their intellectual knowledge?

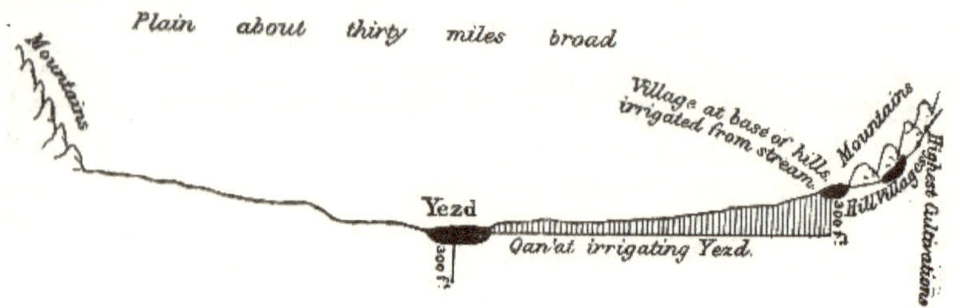

Diagram illustrating the use of the qan'at. Notice that all the cultivation about the hills is irrigated from the snow torrent. Yezd is irrigated by qan'at water, brought in some cases from a point 30 miles distant, for the qan'ats do not go straight to the centre of the plain but make for a low part of the plain from wherever water is found. The 300 ft. well in Yezd is useless for irrigation, there being no lower point than Yezd.

DEHBALA.
A hill village on one of the snow torrents.

CHAPTER II

The population of Yezd can only be guessed at, but probably that of the town proper is between thirty and forty thousand, and that of the town and surrounding villages between fifty and sixty thousand. This little community is insular beyond the insularity of islands. Within two hundred miles there are three sizable cities, Shīrāz, Kirmān, and Isfahān, of which Isfahan is slightly the nearest. When you send a letter to Isfahan from Yezd, if your friend writes by return of post you may get back your answer in a month; although a runner, taking the slightly shorter road by the mountains, could go and return within the week. Travelling in the ordinary way the journey takes eight days there, and eight back.

It is a great pity that within the last two years they have got rid of the native telegraph line. During my journey up six years ago this contrivance was a source of never-failing interest and surprise to me. First of all there were the poles. They were rough sticks, exactly like what a washerwoman in England uses for propping up her clothes-line: I suppose, taking the good line with the bad, there was on the average about one insulator to every three poles; this is without counting the insulators which were hung midway between the poles, apparently by way of ornament. The wire itself was at different levels: in a good many places it lay on the ground, but at others it crossed the road about the level of a horseman's chin. One day in Yezd one of the European residents wanted to send a telegram, and sent to the telegraph office to ask when the line would be up. They sent back a very polite message to say that the trouble was not that the line was down; it was always down: the difficulty was that a camel had stepped upon it.

Of course they do repair the line: we saw a man repairing it. He had a forked stick about half the length of one of the poles on which the line was hung. With this he caught the wire and hitched it on to the nearest fork of the telegraph pole, a procedure which had at any rate the advantage of economy. I think I may say that telegrams by this line never went faster than the post goes in England. The slightest fall of snow or any other similar cause cut the communications altogether, sometimes for a fortnight; and, on similar lines that were a little longer, if you sent a telegram to your destination while you yourself were on a journey, it was a quite common occurrence for the telegraph master at the next town to ask you to carry it yourself as the quickest way of hastening its arrival.

Such an apparatus as this could hardly be expected to prove a great connecting influence. As a matter of fact, the Yezdi regards the Isfahani as a foreigner. When I was leaving Yezd I remember the sensation amongst my servants when they heard that my successor, who was going to take on most of them, wanted to bring an Isfahani butler. Yezdis hardly recognise the bond of a common country at all. There are three connecting links which appeal to them; the link of a common religion; the link of a common family or business, for the family tie is of a character that includes the relation between employé and employer; and lastly, the link of the common town. [3] The bond of fellow-townsmanship is perhaps not considered a very close one, but for all that it is a real link. However, if you were to suggest to a Yezdi that he ought to have something in common with a Bushīrī, irrespective of the question of religion, simply because they both paid taxes to a common king, I very much doubt whether he would understand what you meant, and, if he did, I am quite sure that he would think that you were either joking or a lunatic.

In the vocabulary of the common people it is difficult to find an intelligible word for *country*. There is a word for *empire*, but the natural equivalent in the Persian mind to our expression *country*, meaning fatherland, is *shahr*, which denotes a town, or *vatan*, which is the home-district, and is used in very much the same way. "What is your town?" is the Persian's way of saying, "Where do you come from?" and although he has been taught to call an Englishman *Inglīs*, he almost invariably calls England *Landan*; indeed it is this which we put as an address on all our English letters.

The Yezdi's ideas on the regions beyond his very narrow horizon are distinctly confused. If you begin to talk to him about other places, you are met not by mere ignorance of geography, but by a conception of the surface of the earth that is ludicrously impossible. It is difficult for a European to conceive of a number of towns and villages, containing several millions of people, bedded out over an enormous desert area considerably larger than the whole of France. It is equally difficult for the Yezdi to conceive of a natural and continuous land. Even those who have travelled a little outside Yezd, and have been obliged to modify slightly the Yezdi conception of the universe, have built up their notions of the world's surface upon what seems to us a most peculiar first idea; and they have in most cases clung to far more of their original views than we should believe possible.

The Yezdi's idea of the town as the only geographical and political unit is simply a generalisation from the circumstances of his own city. Yezd is a solitary object rising abruptly out of a vast desert that is about the nearest thing to a vacuum which Nature has yet produced. Then too, the methods by which the Shah retains his half of the government of the country—I say his half, for half of the real control of the people is in the hands of the Mussulman clergy—is in some points similar to the old Roman system of provincial government. The local governor, and not the supreme sovereign, is the real ruler, and he rather than his people is responsible to the head of the State. Of course he is only appointed for a time, and is in constant expectation of recall. Still, while he remains, his power is limited more by the power of the Mohammedan mullās on the one hand, and by the strength and number of his subordinate officials and guards on the other, and much less by the orders and authority that he receives from Tehran. But it is true that the Yezdi exaggerates the separateness of his town, for he hardly recognises the actual limitations to the Governor's power made and enforced by the Shah. Of course it is thoroughly understood that the Governor only holds his office by the Shah's appointment; but it is very difficult for the Yezdi to realise that that appointment, while it lasts, is to anything short of autocracy. So to him the local Government is *the* Government, and the local Governor the real ruler of his country, that is to say of the district surrounding his town; and it would puzzle him if you were to tell him that there were people in this world, living together in one sphere of government, who were not resident in one town, or in the district that belonged to it.

It may be urged that I am speaking of the uneducated and ignorant class, but there are very few in a town like Yezd who are not uneducated and ignorant, and even those who have superadded a certain degree of knowledge, have, in almost all cases, retained the majority of their preconceptions. Persians are very slow in seeing a contradiction; consequently, I believe that this conception of the universe, which is certainly accepted by the ordinary Yezdi, is with small modifications very general even among the slightly travelled or educated classes. Nor should a student of the mental attitude of a people ignore the curious ideas that are to be found amongst the women. One who had moved a great deal amongst the women of Yezd, assured me that they were almost invariably under the impression that the less familiar words occurring in the Persian translation of the Scriptures were English, and that it was a common thing for a woman who was accustomed to the European pronunciation of Persian, to be referred to as knowing the language of the Ferangis. Such people would, of course, fail to comprehend the possibility of a linguistic barrier very much greater than the somewhat considerable difference of dialect which separates them from their neighbours in Isfahan. That such a state of mind would be equally possible amongst the men I do not for a moment suppose, but if this is the view of the women, one may be sure that there is a view of the Ferangi stranger, more or less approximating to it, amongst many of the ignorant hobbledehoys and young fellows, who contribute the largest share to the character of a fanatical Persian crowd.

Now the people of Yezd are quite ready after a due interval to extend the citizenship to strangers from other towns, provided that the newcomers intend to stay, and are ready to enter into the life of the community. The Kāshīs from Kāshān, the Shīrāzīs from Shīrāz, the Lārīs from Lāristān, and the Rashtīs from Rasht, are all well-known Yezd families, and are not by any means regarded as foreigners. Also the Yezd community includes persons of three or four different religions. There are in the town fourteen hundred Parsi houses, the inhabitants of which are Zoroastrian. There is also a smaller colony of Jews. The remainder are Mohammedans; but a considerable number of these belong to the Behāī sect, and are considered rank heretics. The Parsis, though greatly oppressed in the past, and still liable to some disabilities, have of late years become wealthy and prosperous. The Jews are in some ways less restricted than the Parsis; but, as they are still wretchedly poor, they are really much more down-trodden. That religious bigotry still exists among the Mussulmans in Yezd has only lately been made perfectly plain by the ghastly massacre of the Behāīs in the summer of 1903; but Mohammedan bigotry in Persia is by no means without limitations. It is spasmodic in its action, nor does it entirely obliterate every other feeling.

A few years ago Yezd had the reputation of being one of the most bigoted of the towns of Persia. The presence of the Zoroastrian remnant, who were subject to the grossest persecution, served only to keep alive the fire of religious hatred; and the community of Jews in a lesser degree had the same effect. The stories of the way in which the Parsis were bullied and persecuted are interesting, as showing, amongst other things, the intense childishness of the Persian Mussulman. The atmosphere of the town seems to have resembled, as indeed it still resembles, that of a preparatory school for little boys. Up to 1895 no Parsi was allowed to carry an umbrella. Even during the time that I was in Yezd they could not carry one in town. Up to 1895 there was a strong prohibition upon eye-glasses and spectacles; up to 1885 they were prevented from wearing rings; their girdles had to be made of rough canvas, but after 1885 any white material was permitted. Up to 1896 the Parsis were obliged to twist their turbans instead of folding them. Up to about 1898 only brown, grey, and yellow were allowed for the *qabā* or *arkhālūq* (body garments), but after that all colours were permitted, except blue, black, bright red, or green. There was also a prohibition against white stockings, and up to about 1880 the Parsis had to wear a special kind of peculiarly hideous shoe with a broad, turned-up toe. Up to 1885 they had to wear a torn cap. Up to about 1880 they had to wear tight knickers, self-coloured, instead of trousers. Up to 1891 all Zoroastrians had to walk in town, and even in the desert they had to dismount if they met a Mussulman of any rank whatsoever. During the time that I was in Yezd they were allowed to ride in the desert, and only had to dismount if they met a big Mussulman. There were other similar dress restrictions too numerous and trifling to mention. Then the houses of both the Parsis and the Jews, with the surrounding walls, had to be built so low that the top could be reached by a Mussulman with his hand extended; they might, however, dig down below the level of the road. The walls had to be splashed with white round the door. Double doors, the common form of Persian door, were forbidden, also rooms containing three or more windows. *Bad-girs* were still forbidden to the Parsis while we were in Yezd, but in 1900 one of the bigger Parsi merchants gave a large present to the Governor and to the chief *mujtahid* (Mohammedan priest) to be allowed to build one. Upper rooms were also forbidden.

Up to about 1860 Parsis could not engage in trade. They used to hide things in their cellar rooms, and sell them secretly. They can now trade in the caravanserais or hostelries, but not in the bazaars, nor may they trade in linen drapery. Up to 1870 they were not permitted to have a school for their children.

The amount of the *jazīya*, or tax upon infidels, differed according to the wealth of the individual Parsi, but it was never less than two *tomāns*. A *toman* is now worth about three shillings and eight pence, but it used to be worth much more. Even now, when money has much depreciated, it represents a labourer's wage for ten days. The money had to be paid on the spot, when the *farrash*, who was acting as collector, met the man. The *farrash* was at liberty to do what he liked when collecting *jaziya*. The man was not even allowed to go home and fetch the money, but was at once beaten until it was given. About 1865 a *farrāsh* collecting this tax tied a man to a dog, and gave a blow to each in turn.

About 1891 a *mujtahid* caught a Zoroastrian merchant wearing white stockings in one of the public squares of the town. He ordered the man to be beaten and the stockings taken off. About 1860 a man of seventy went to the bazaars in white trousers of rough canvas. They hit him about a good deal, took off his trousers, and sent him home with them under his arm. Sometimes Parsis would be made to stand on one leg in a *mujtahid's* house until they consented to pay a considerable sum of money. Occasionally, however, the childish mockery that pervaded the persecuting ordinances enabled the Zoroastrians to evade the disabilities proposed. For instance, as the Jews had to wear a patch on the *qaba*, or coat, the *mujtahids* in about 1880 tried to make the Parsis wear an obvious patch on the shirt. Muhammad Hasan Khan was then Governor, and Mulla Bahrām of Khurramshār, a Parsi, asked him to arrange that his people should have three days' respite to get the patches ready. During these three days the Parsi women set to work, and made a neat embroidered border round the neck and opening of the shirt. This the Parsis exhibited as the required patch; and as it was very obvious, and was certainly an insertion, there was really nothing more to be said. In Yezd a small score like this counts for more than does a firman of the Shah.

In the reign of the late Shah Nāsiru'd Dīn, Mānukjī Limjī, a British Parsi from India, was for a long while in Tehran as Parsi representative. Almost all the Parsi disabilities were withdrawn, the *jaziya*, the clothes restrictions, the riding restrictions, and those with regard to houses, but the law of inheritance was not altered, according to which a Parsi who has become a Mussulman takes precedence of his Zoroastrian brothers and sisters. The *jaziya* was actually remitted, and also some of the restrictions as to houses, but the rest of the firman was a dead letter.

In 1898 the present Shah, Muzaffaru'd Dīn, gave a firman to Dīnyār, the present *Qalāntar* of the Parsi *Anjuman*, or Committee, revoking all the remaining Parsi disabilities, and also declaring it unlawful to use fraud or deception in making conversions of Parsis to Islam. This firman does not appear to have had any effect at all.

About 1883, after the firman of Nāsiru'd Dīn Shah had been promulgated, one of the Parsis, Rustami Ardishīri Dīnyār, built in Kūcha Biyuk, one of the villages near Yezd, a house with an upper room, slightly above the height to which the Parsis used to be limited. He heard that the Mussulmans were going to kill him, so he fled by night to Tehran. They killed another Parsi, Tīrandāz, in mistake for him, but did not destroy the house.

So the great difficulty was not to get the law improved, but rather to get it enforced. When Manukji was at Yezd, about 1870, two Parsis were attacked by two Mussulmans outside the town, and one was killed, the other being terribly wounded, as they had tried to cut off his head. The Governor brought the criminals to Yezd, but did nothing to them. Manukji then got leave to take them to Tehran. The Prime Minister, however, told him that no Mussulman would be killed for a *Zardūshtī*, or Zoroastrian, and that they would only be bastinadoed. About this time Manukji enquired whether it was true that the blood-price of a *Zardushti* was to be seven *tomans*. He got back the official reply that it was to be a little over.

The Yezd Parsis have been helped considerably by agents from Bombay, who are British subjects, and of late years things have slightly improved. About 1885, a *Seyid*, that is, a descendant of Muhammad, killed a *Zardushti* woman in Yezd. Ibrāhīm Qalīl Khān took him, and, by order of the Zillu's Sultān, Prince Governor of Isfahan, and elder brother of the Shah, killed him before daybreak. When the Mohammedan mullas heard of it in the morning, they gave orders for a general slaughter of the Parsis. Many of the Parsis were injured, but none killed. Then in 1899 the Sahāmu'l Mulk, at the commencement of his governorship of Yezd, killed a Mussulman servant of the Mushīru'l Mamālik for a criminal assault upon a Zoroastrian woman. This man was not a Seyid, which made the matter more simple. Just before, when the Mushīru'l Mamālik was temporary Governor, Isfandiār, the Parsi schoolmaster at Taft, one of the large Yezd villages, and Salāmat, another Parsi, were killed by two *lūtīs* (roughs) without reason. One of these *lutis* was a Seyid. Both were sent to Tehran, and a *mujtahid* went up with them to ask for their release. The Shah ordered the Seyid's release, but the fate of the other is not known. That the Seyid was not much intimidated is certain, as in the August of 1901, when I was in Taft, he used to wander about with other *lutis* quite openly.

During the last nine or ten years the governors in Yezd have been much stronger, and they have, generally speaking, been friendly to the Parsis. The Parsis are an industrious and intelligent people, and they have become in Yezd a wealthy community. Also there is an extremely wealthy Parsi in Tehran, Arbāb Jamshīd, who is probably more able to influence the Persian Government in favour of his countrymen than are the Indian Parsis from Bombay. Nowadays no governor who wants to remain in Yezd can afford to leave the Parsi community out of his calculations. The real advance made by the Parsi colony seems to date from the second term of government of the Jalālu'd Daula, eldest son of the Zillu's Sultān, Governor of Isfahan. The Parsis themselves also put down a great deal of the improvement in their circumstances to the spread of the Behāī faith, and certainly, although a semi-secret sect, the Behāīs individually plead openly for a general religious liberty and toleration. Naturally such a movement has been of considerable assistance to the Parsis. As an indication of the influence of the Parsis, it is interesting to notice that during the late Behāī massacres, immediately there was talk of an attack on the Parsi quarter, the Mussulman clergy applied themselves to suppressing the movement.

Although the Jews are very much weaker and poorer, they have their place in the social organisation of the town, and the contempt in which they are held does not prevent the Yezdis from recognising their right to a kind of citizenship. Their religion of course is held in much greater respect than that of the Parsis, for they are people of the Book, and although the Persian Shiahs granted the Zoroastrians a certain share in this status, when they allowed them to continue in the country on the same terms as Jews and Christians, the ordinary Yezdi of to-day hesitates considerably before he allows that Zoroaster was in any sense a prophet.

I myself have met Mussulmans serving in a menial capacity in Parsi houses; I have entertained Parsis of standing and Mussulmans of standing together on public occasions; and I have no hesitation in saying that even the bigoted Mussulman recognises the bond of common citizenship, although it is certainly true that on most occasions he prefers the bond of religion. Still, a Persian's religious feeling, even when it seems to amount to fanatical bigotry, is generally so connected with self-interest, that, when it is disconnected from thoughts of profit, it is difficult to know how much influence it will possess with him.

It is certainly a fact that a year or two ago, when an Isfahani Seyid came and preached in the Yezd mosques against painted trays, Manchester cottons, bank-notes, and Bibles, the Yezdi Mussulmans gave him the cold shoulder, and treated him as a foreigner who had intruded himself into their domestic concerns.

People were surprised at this happening in the city which a few years before had been regarded as one of the most fanatical in the whole of Persia. As a matter of fact, the so-called fanaticism of Yezd was two-thirds of it non-religious in character. There was an element of turbulency, produced by a series of weak governors; there was a real religious element; and there was an element of insularity, utterly unconnected with creed and doctrine. In spite of the smallness of the Christian colony, which even at present consists of only eighteen Europeans, to which may be added twenty-two Armenians (the households of men in European employment), the people of the town which is after all not large, had soon become familiarised with this little settlement as a Yezd institution. Then the insular spirit came to be enlisted on the side of the Ferangis, and, the turbulence produced by weak governorship being eliminated, there was only the religious difficulty left.

There have only been Europeans in Yezd for some twelve years. The early arrivals were a bank manager and a merchant's agent. The work of the Church Missionary Society has been established there for some six years, and the English telegraph clerk has been there for about a year. Now all the members of the colony have contributed something to the life of the town, and all the Europeans have worked together with marked cordiality and harmony. Both of these things have certainly had a great effect in hastening the establishment of the colony in the town, and in winning for it the support of the Yezdis' insular prejudices. The merchants are distinctly glad of the bank, and of the resident agent from a responsible Manchester firm. The people have learnt to value the Medical Mission; and the schools, though they appeal to a smaller class, appeal equally strongly.

Even the directly spiritual work of a Mission is granted an established position in the town by the natives, if it is partially in connection with the Christian community. Having granted a community right of residence no Mohammedan would deny them the right of religious observance. Indeed this would be expected to exist as a matter of course.

It is quite true that Christian missions in Persia do not possess the treaty right to make converts from Mohammedanism. At the same time, it must be remembered that Persians are much more inclined to regard custom than law, nor are they used to the accurate observance of a fine distinction. All that can be said is that, at present, the right of a Christian missionary to baptize a Mussulman is in Yezd by no means established, but that his right to live and work and preach in the town as, primarily, the *mujtahid* of the Ferangis, and secondarily, an accepted Yezd teacher, is practically recognised by all. This point seems to have been arrived at chiefly through the acceptance of the entire European colony as unitedly Christian and as a real part of the town. Things that have helped us to arrive at it have been the usefulness of the various branches of work engaged in by the Europeans, their general straightforwardness and honesty of life, combined with their ready co-operation in Christian effort; also the extreme acceptability of the work of the medical missions, and the linking of the clerical work with the life of the town through the medium of schools. To these must be added the smallness of Yezd, which makes it impossible for the population consistently to ignore or refuse to assimilate any important band of workers that can maintain a residence at all prolonged within its walls, and the insularity which makes it impossible to refuse altogether to champion what has become part of the town. Also we must not forget the natural proneness of the Shiah to religious speculation, and the special ferment of religious ideas at present prevailing throughout Persia. This, however, is a matter that will be dealt with at length, later on.

A curious incident occurred in Yezd not long ago, that will perhaps serve to point to the extraordinary way in which the Europeans have in the mind of the Yezdi become an established part of the town population, with rights and privileges similar to those possessed by the native section of the townsfolk. One of the European residents had received a threatening letter from a young Mussulman, whom he had dismissed from his employ; and he had paid as little attention to the matter as it deserved. It so happened that the next day he came to our house for a week's visit, I being a clerical missionary; and the dismissed servant then spread the report through the bazaars that his master was frightened, and had taken sanctuary with his *mujtahid*, this being a common Mussulman custom when danger is apprehended either from *lutis* or from the law. Not only was the report believed, but one of the other Europeans was obliged to give up a visit which he had intended to pay us, as he was a business man, and his credit might have been temporarily shaken.

A similar story is told by Canon Bruce, of an experience in Isfahan. Though in some ways more curious, it is, however, less convincing with regard to the particular moral to which I am attempting to point, since the Canon was then working largely amongst the Armenian Christians of Julfa, who are a considerable colony, and subjects of the Shah. The Roman Catholic Armenian priests, who were also working amongst the Armenian Christians, got the chief Mussulman *mujtahid* of Isfahan, of which Julfa is a suburb, to summon Canon Bruce to his house. The *mujtahid*, they said, was, after all, the chief religious authority in the place, and Canon Bruce was as much a heretic in Christianity as the Babis were in Islam. This quaint summons was actually issued, and the Mussulman *mujtahid* required Canon Bruce to defend himself against the charge of preaching incorrect Christian doctrine. This, of course, was an acceptance of Canon Bruce's position; but the acceptance of the position of a clerical missionary in a place where there were only eight or nine households belonging to Christian races, European or Armenian, is stranger still.

The possibility of such a thing ought, however, to encourage us with regard to the future of missionary work in isolated and apparently bigoted Persian towns, and also to make missionaries realise the immense value of the co-operation of Christian residents, and the necessity of attending fully to their spiritual needs.

CHAPTER III

We have seen that the Yezdis have long been accustomed to have in their midst professors of three distinct religions, the Jewish, the Zoroastrian and the Mohammedan. But as the Jews are neither numerous nor influential, and the Zoroastrian Parsis, though more numerous than the Jews, are nevertheless not more than a tithe of the population, the religion that chiefly demands our attention is Mohammedanism, which is the established faith of Persia. The Mohammedanism of Persia is not quite the same as that of India or Turkey, and the Persians call themselves *Shiahs* or nonconformists. In Persia there is one creed of nonconformity which is there accepted as orthodox, so those professing this creed will for the future in these pages be called Shiahs without further qualification.

It must, however, be remembered that the name Shiah is not properly confined to this one sect, and also that this sect itself, like other nonconformist bodies, has always shown a great tendency to subdivide. In Persia besides Shiahs, that is the more orthodox Shiahs, there has always been one other smaller sect of Mohammedans attracting general attention. At present the dissenting doctrine most widely taught is that of the Behāīs, who have laid hold of the popular imagination, partly because of their great steadfastness under the most terrible persecutions, partly because of the somewhat popular nature of their teaching, but chiefly because Persia is now being brought into rather closer touch with Europe, and the people as a whole feel that the teaching of the Shiah mullas needs to be modified if Islam is to be preserved. I think one may go further, and say that there is at present in Persia a period of enquiry and spiritual awakening, which gives a special opportunity, not only to Mohammedan sectaries, but also to Christian missionaries. Later on further allusion will be made to these Behāīs, but we must not forget that our first task is not so much the study of the complex religious systems of Persia, as the analysis of those religious influences to which the Yezdi has been subjected.

The ordinary Yezdi Mussulman is descended partly from the original Aryan inhabitants of Persia, and partly from their Arabian conquerors: but the enormous difference in character that exists between him and the purely Aryan Parsi is certainly due less to race and more to religion, for the *jadīds*, or converts from Parsiism, often develop all the Mussulman characteristics in a few generations, without the slightest admixture of race. So before attempting to describe the character of the people, it will be necessary to pay as much attention to the religious ideas that have been brought to bear upon them as we have already paid to the nature of their country and the seclusion of their town life. Some aspects of the Yezdi's religion will be left to a future chapter, and we must at present content ourselves with trying to understand the essential nature of Islam, particularly dwelling on those points of Mohammed's teaching and example which seem to have produced most impression on the Persian mind. To do this we must divest ourselves of all pre-judgments of the prophet's life and doctrine, and simply study the facts of history, remembering that the conception of Islam which is to be found amongst the Sunnis of India and Turkey cannot be allowed to pass unchallenged, for the Mohammedan world is by no means unanimous about it; and also that the well-known European theory, that there was a difference in Mohammed's aims and objects in Mecca and Medina, and that the Meccan period rather than the Medinan indicates the essential idea of Mohammedanism, is one which no educated Mussulman would for a moment tolerate. As for the still more favourable views that have been lately brought forward by European authors, I can only pass on a story that was told me of an educated Mussulman in India who had been shown such a treatise. "This gentleman, Sahib," he said, as he handed back the volume, "appears to know very little about his own religion, and absolutely nothing about ours."

I myself went to Persia with the intention of making the most of the good points of the religious systems of the country. With regard to the Parsis I was not disappointed. Like many other missionaries, I started with the idea that I should find these people possessed of a great many radically wrong notions about the nature and power of God, which were essential to their religion. I now believe that I was wrong, and I have never heard my right-hand man, Mihraban, who is himself a Parsi, and also one of the most sincere and earnest Christians whom I have ever met, speak one word against the real groundwork of Zoroastrianism. In this religion it is not unteaching but teaching that is required to lead the people to Christ; but, in Mohammedanism, in spite of its greater pretensions, almost every apparent truth crumbles into mere truism or actual falsity the moment that you try to make it the basis of anything practical. Also the more I read of the life of Mohammed, the more convinced I am that the radical rottenness of the system is due to his original teaching. Perhaps this may be a confession of narrowness, but one cannot be broad all round. Unless we are going to deny the iniquity and wickedness of modern Islam, we shall have to believe that somebody is to blame; and, if it is not Mohammed, I suppose it must be either the mullas or the Mussulman laity. I do not know why we should expend all our breadth on the big people: I myself have some sympathy with the little ones: and I firmly believe that the difficulties in the Islam of to-day are due rather to the essential wrongness of the system than to its corruption by the masses.

Mohammed was born in Mecca towards the end of the sixth century. He was a member of the important family who had charge of the Ka'aba, which was a heathen temple that the Meccans had attempted to make a common meeting-ground for the whole of Arabia, by including within its limits the idols and symbols of worship that were respected by the different tribes. Some of these tribes had adopted Christianity and Judaism; so pictures even of Jewish and Christian saints were to be found within the walls of the Meccan temple.

The Mussulman historians of Mohammed's life tell us that there had been in Arabia, for some years before the prophet came forward, a set of reformers called *Hanīfs*, who seem to have been half political and half religious, but to have been all of them convinced that some form of religion, purer than that represented by the Ka'aba, was needed to unite Arabia against its common foes. Some of these *Hanifs* ended by adopting Christianity or Judaism; others were inclined to the adoption of a more essentially national form of monotheism, which should retain the Ka'aba as its centre. The most notable of the latter party was Zaid ibn Amr, a man so much admired by Mohammed that he declared him a prophet, and in other ways professed his complete acceptation of his principles and teaching.

Mohammed by his marriage with Khadīja was certainly introduced into this set of reformers. Waraka ibn Nawfal was one of the most prominent *Hanifs*, and we have indisputable evidence that he was one of Khadija's most intimate friends, both at the time of her marriage, and also at the time when her husband received his first revelation. Mohammed himself had been from childhood of a hysterical disposition, and was subject to fits, during which he saw visions, which on recovering consciousness he was able to recollect; consequently while in this company he became convinced that he was the expected prophet who was to bind Arabia together by a politico-religious system.

In placing himself at the head of the *Hanif* movement, Mohammed probably gave more prominence to the political aspect than had most of the former and less successful leaders. This is brought out by Koelle in his life of Mohammed; and indeed it is obvious that the man who could allow an unbelieving friend, even though a close relation, to play the important part in the building of his church that Abbās played in the second meeting on the eminence, was primarily a politician rather than a religious reformer: for it was Abbas who on that occasion first proposed the oath that may almost be called the basis of Islam. A critical study of Mohammed's early dealings with the Arabians brings us to a similar conclusion.

Of the other stories collected by Koelle from Mussulman sources to prove this point, perhaps the most forcible is that of the discussion between the prophet, his uncle, Abu Tālib, under whose protection he was then living, and Abu Jahl. Abu Talib called his nephew and said to him, "Thou seest the nobles of thy people are assembled here to concede to thee certain things, and, in return, to receive concessions from thee." Mohammed made this reply: "Well, then, give me a word whereby the Arabs may be governed and the Persians subjugated." Abu Jahl responded to this request in the name of his fellow-elders by saying: "Thou shalt have ten words." But Mohammed setting him right, and indicating what kind of word in his opinion could alone answer the purpose, rejoined: "Say, 'There is no God except Allah!' and renounce what you worship besides Him." This story Koelle quotes from Ibn Ishāk, the earliest and most trustworthy biographer.

Certainly the movement from paganism to monotheism, which took place in Arabia in those days, was in itself a fine thing; and it was accompanied by much sincerity and religious zeal. It is also obvious that Mohammed possessed a personality peculiarly attractive to the Arabian, and that this, as well as his enthusiasm on the subject of his mission, had the effect of attracting many to the cause.

But not only did Mohammed pay much more regard to politics than can be possibly excused, he also accepted the religious and ethical teaching of the *Hanifs* only in the most superficial manner; and, under the cover of verbal conformity, retained as much as possible of the original pagan ideas in which he had been reared. The result is that his followers are still to be found possessed of what seems at first sight to be correct doctrine upon fundamentals, and yet are unable to advance by its assistance along the path of light and progress.

The popular idea, that fanatical intolerance of all professors of other religions is an essential and fundamental principle in Mohammedanism, cannot be maintained. The paganism of Mecca was distinctly latitudinarian, so Mohammed accepted in full the sacred books of the Jews and Christians, as would have seemed natural to an Arabian of that age, especially to a monotheistic teacher who was closely connected with the Ka'aba. This does not mean that he in any way apprehended the meaning of Judaism and Christianity. The doctrine of the perpetuity of the moral law never seems to have entered into his mind, even in the most elementary form. He wished to say that he had himself received a revelation superseding all former ones by the mandate of God, and he did not wish to make trouble by pronouncing other religions to be false, without absolute necessity. His real object was to unite the Arabs by a reformed religion, and at first he regarded his mission as a purely national one. Whatever were his ultimate designs upon the Jews and Christians in Arabia, he intentionally conveyed to them the impression that, if they recognised him as a prophet to others, he would be content without their accepting him themselves. Indeed, while he was still at Mecca, he was even uncertain whether the idolaters who accepted him might not be allowed to retain some of their idols as intermediaries between themselves and Allah. He went so far on one occasion as to actually effect a reconciliation on this basis; but as such a concession must have greatly damaged his influence with those who were favourably disposed to the *Hanif* movement, he afterwards repudiated the transaction, and declared that he had acted under the influence of the devil. His work in Mecca was not very successful; and the opposition he encountered was so strong that he had at last to begin to make attempts to start work in some other place, and he was finally successful in making a fresh beginning in Medina. Here he was able to take advantage of a family connection with some of the principal citizens, and also of a long-standing rivalry between Medina and Mecca. Although the movement in Mecca had not been widely successful, Mohammed had gathered amongst his followers several really prominent men. Consequently, the people of Medina, although divided on the subject of his prophetic mission, were unanimous as to the advisability of receiving him and his followers into their town. Settled in Medina, Mohammed's fortunes underwent a change. The chieftancy of the tribe to which his grandmother had belonged fell vacant, and, as most of the members of this tribe had become Mussulmans, Mohammed had no difficulty in himself becoming their chief. Considering himself restrained by no preconception or former revelation of the moral law, he was able, without dropping for one moment his pretensions to prophethood, to use every means of fraud and violence which seemed conducive to his political end. As Koelle has pointed out, there is no reason to suppose that his principles in any way changed, but under the altered conditions and environment the utterly non-ethical theory of revelation held by the prophet became more apparent. This is perhaps most clearly brought out by his utterly unscrupulous dealing with the Jews, and also by the story of Zaid and Zainab, in all which affairs Mohammed professed himself to be acting under Divine direction, nor is it at all obvious that he did not actually believe it. Finally, before his death, he succeeded in establishing his religion and political system throughout the whole of Arabia.

Of course it was impossible for a movement like this to take place without rival prophets appearing in other parts of the country. Two of these appeared during Mohammed's lifetime, and he thought it best to guard against future schisms of a similar kind by declaring himself the last of the prophets. Exactly what he meant by this is not very clear: if the almost universal voice of Islam is to be accepted, he did not mean that he was the last divinely appointed teacher, for all Mussulmans look forward to the coming of a Mehdi or Mahdi, who, together with Jesus, the son of Mary, is to appear in the last days, and spread the doctrines of Islam throughout the world. Orthodox Mussulmans, however, always look upon Mohammed as the last great *sāhibi kitāb*, or book-bearer.

The ordinary Sunnis, who are the largest and best-known Mussulman sect, assert that, as a matter of fact, since the time of Mohammed, no divinely-appointed teacher has as yet appeared. The Khalīfs were in their eyes simply appointed by the congregation, and the four great writers of the *sunnat*, which is to them the only authoritative commentary upon the doctrines of Islam, were only learned and saintly men. Now, they hold, these doctrines can only be learnt from this book, and from the *Qurān* itself; for the *mujtahid* or high mulla, capable of giving authoritative decisions on moot points, no longer exists.

The Shiahs have very different tenets. Mohammed according to their teaching was the first of a hierarchic dynasty of thirteen, consisting of himself and the twelve great Imāms, of whom the first was Ali, the son-in-law of the prophet, and who were all as certainly divinely appointed as Mohammed himself. Mohammed is only the last great book-bearer, and therefore the founder of the present era. The last of the Imams was the Mehdi, who according to the Sunnis has not yet been born, but according to the Shiahs appeared long ago. This man did not die, but disappeared, remaining at first accessible to his followers through the medium of four successive Bābs, or gates of knowledge, who were in touch with him during his concealment. Like the Imams, the Babs came to an end, for the last of them refused to appoint a successor. All this of course is very ancient history.

The Shiahs have their own traditionists, for they reject the *sunnat* altogether. Between the traditions of the Shiahs and the Sunnis there is not much to choose: there is a certain amount of historical fact embodied in both, and there is also a great deal of absolute nonsense. However, many otherwise orthodox Shiahs either reject the traditions altogether, or interpret them allegorically. There is more freedom of interpretation amongst the Shiahs than amongst the Sunnis: indeed many Shiahs believe that some of the most objectionable chapters of the *Quran* describing the delights of heaven are entirely parabolic. Of course with *mujtahids* (supposed to be able to pronounce authoritatively on moot points) scattered all over Persia, the fixity of doctrine that prevails amongst Mohammedans of Sunni countries would be impossible.

The tenets of the Shiahs are not derogatory to the mission of Mohammed, or to the position of the *Quran*, but they make the solitary figure of the prophet stand out much less prominently. For instance, if a Persian is told that his religion possesses nothing corresponding to the vicarious sacrifice of Christ, he will invariably reply by pointing to the martyrdom of the Imam Husain. Also the Mehdi, or occult Imam, is not the future, but the present ruler of Islam; and so he is in some ways as important a personage as the original prophet. Not very long ago the Shah of Persia used to pay rent for his palace to the Mehdi, the money going to the *mujtahids* as the representatives of the Imam: I do not know whether this practice is still continued, but the theory on which it was based is certainly not extinct. Again there is a common saying that the Imam Ali is present in the heart of the true believer, but I think it is only regarded by the ordinary Yezdi as a poetical expression. The point to be noted is that the saying is always about Ali, not about Mohammed. Shiahs invoke the Imams Ali and Husain very much more frequently than they invoke Mohammed; and though the inscription over a Persian mosque should be, "*Yā Ali, Yā Muhammad,*" that is, "O Ali! O Mohammed!" the "*Yā Muhammad*" is often omitted and the "*Yā Ali*" left to stand alone. The excuse is sometimes brought forward that Mohammed is too great for constant invocation. Considering the way in which the Shiah uses the name of God, this must, I think, be regarded as a mere excuse for a habit due to wholly different causes.

This extreme attachment to the Imams is probably due to two things. In the first place, there can be no doubt that the cause of Ali and his sons was taken up in Persia as an outlet to national jealousy, for the Aryan converts were not sorry when a pretext occurred for differentiating themselves from the majority of their Arab conquerors. In the Shiah religion the early Khalifs, who ruled Islam while the holy Imams were still alive, are held up to the bitterest execration, and Omar in particular, who, by the way, was the conqueror of Persia, takes much the same place in the Shiah system that Judas Iscariot does in the Christian.

SMALL SQUARE IN YEZD.

To the left is a small Nakhl, and in the centre a
mosque door with the inscription "Ya Ali."

Secondly, the influence of sects of mystics, professedly Mohammedan but having in their doctrines a distinctly pantheistic tendency, must be remembered. Ancient Persia was full of pantheism, and when it became Mussulman the inclination towards such teaching still continued, for the broader views held by the Shiahs as to freedom of interpretation in reading the *Quran* gave a possible status in the country to very heretical sects. These Persian mystics often preferred to make the Imams, especially Ali, at least as prominent in their systems as Mohammed, whose teaching was more difficult to bend to their purposes; and although the ordinary Yezdi is certainly not a pantheist, they have undoubtedly intensified his enthusiasm for the personalities of the Imams, and through their poetry they have familiarised him with religious expressions of a somewhat unorthodox character. This is in some ways an advantage to the missionary, but he must beware that it does not give him a false view of the progress that he is making.

As to the theory of the divinely appointed Imamate it might be urged that the retention of the whole glory of the early sainthood for the close relations and descendants of the prophet is an excess of zeal that Mohammed would have greatly approved. However this may be, the doctrine is not obviously opposed to Mohammedanism.

The Shiahs are certainly much laxer than the Sunnis with regard to some of the commandments of the *Qurān*. Painting, and the making of figures is considered by the Sunnis to be a violation of the law against idolatry. There is, however, a regular school of Persian painting; and clay models of men, animals and demons, as well as rag dolls, are given to the children as toys. The protests made by the mullas against these things are very faint. They are rather louder in their denunciations of all forms of music, which amongst orthodox Mohammedans is supposed to have no purpose but the exciting of the passions. As to the drinking of wine and spirits, the avoidance of the regular Mohammedan fast in the month of Ramazān, and the omission of the prescribed prayers, the Shiah mullas take a view which is at least intelligible. To begin with, such things do not amount to infidelity unless they are done wilfully and consistently. A formal acceptation of the whole of the ordinances is demanded. There must be no drunkenness in the streets, no eating in Ramazan when anybody is near unless a legitimate excuse can be brought forward, and if prayers have not been said men must say that they have said them. Further than this external government does not go; and as a matter of fact many irreligious Persians secretly drink themselves drunk in their houses, forget to say their prayers regularly, and make up what would, if true, be valid excuses for not keeping the fast in Ramazan. Such people are well aware that they are liable to punishment, but they also know that, unless they prove disloyal to Islam by accepting some other faith, they are not in any great danger. It is true that every now and again the mullas incite the people to join them in cleansing the land of infidelity, and on such occasions sectaries like the Babis, and those who are supposed to sympathise with them, may greatly suffer, but those who have been merely lax in their observance of Islam are apt to make up for their past deficiencies by a peculiar show of zeal.

It may be asked whether the mullas in Persia are justified in making no more persistent efforts to enforce Mohammedan law, and whether their winking at such irregularities is not in itself disloyalty to the system of Islam. Probably it would be easy for them to show that they were justified by the example of Mohammed himself. If Mohammed enforced a much stricter discipline in the town where he was himself present—a matter which I think is open to doubt—it would be almost impossible to maintain that he caused such discipline to be enforced among the Arab tribes. These tribes were generally accepted through the medium of their chief, who usually came to Mohammed in person, had a short interview with him, part of which was devoted to political subjects, and often went back to his tribe on the same day. It is true that Mohammed made a distinction between hypocrites—

munāfiqīn, and true believers, but he generally meant by hypocrites people who were not really on his side against others, and here the ordinary Shiah is unimpeachable.

The fact is that Islam contains much more than an assortment of commandments. Otherwise it would never have impressed its adherents in so distinct and remarkable a manner with special characteristics. The central idea of the religion is that we are all under the dominion of an invisible and absolutely powerful God, Who has created all things, and has willed and ordained everything both good and evil that is to be found in the universe. It is true that there is a Shiah dogma against the extreme predestinarianism which characterises the Sunni creed, but I do not believe that it has in the least affected the fatalistic view of the ordinary people. In Islam God may be called good because it is our duty to accept as good whatever He does, and He may also be called by other names according to the character of His known actions towards us; but His own nature is absolutely different from that of man; consequently nothing can be known of His moral character beyond the fact of certain explicit actions. This God from time to time sends to the world prophets, whose duty is to teach mankind the doctrine of His unity, the necessity of worship, and the necessity of doing what is for the time being His will. According to the popular opinion there have been a hundred and forty-four thousand of these prophets, but of this number only a few have been authorised to publish a new code of human duty. Those so authorised are known as book-bearers, and Adam, Seth, Enoch, Abraham, Moses, David, Jesus, and Mohammed were all of this class. The Behāīs add the name of Behāu'llah after that of Mohammed. These book-bearers are always marked by the possession of some sort of supernatural powers appealing to the intellect, and also, in the case of the latter ones, by the fulfilment of signs mentioned by the former prophets. Obedience to them is rewarded by various degrees of bliss in Heaven, disobedience is punished by Hell. The prophet must conform to previous revelations in the assertion of God's unity, invisibility and omnipotence, but it is not necessary that there should be any coherence between the directions about human action as set forth in successive dispensations, nor is any difference made between ceremonial and moral commandments.

This central doctrine of Mohammedanism concerns God, the prophet, man and creation; so we come across it under four names, giving the four possible points of view. First of all there is the name of *tauhīd*, or assertion of the Divine unity. The Mussulman means by this very much more than the mere assertion that God is a single Being. He includes in it the doctrine of the invisibility of God and of His absolutely separate nature, and it appears to clash with the Christian conception in two important particulars. There is an absolute denial of the statement, upon which most Christians more or less consciously base their belief in the perpetuity and absolute nature of the law of human morals, that "in the image of God created He man." Consequently we shall afterwards find that in Islam there is no belief in the permanency of the moral law, for nothing is thought by the Mussulman to be necessarily permanent except things connected with the nature of God; and as our nature differs entirely from that of the Creator the law given for it cannot be necessarily permanent. There is also in reality a fundamental contradiction of Christian doctrine in the Mohammedan's rendering of the statement that God is a single Being. This is best explained by a simple illustration. Supposing a man were to say, "London is one place," it is conceivable that he might mean one of two things. Either he might mean that the City of London was the only true London, and that there was no other part of the town in Middlesex or Surrey that ought to be called by the same name; or he might mean that the whole of those places which go by the name of the County of London are in reality only one place; and these two statements are not similar statements with a slight difference, but they are absolutely contradictory. So the Christian says there is only one God, by which he means to assert the unity of the all-good Creator, the all-good Personality Who was revealed as the Son, and the all-good Spirit Who is the only source of good in the heart. As God to the Christian means the All-good, what he needs is a doctrine that asserts the essential unity of the All-good wherever he finds it. The Christian is of course not a pantheist, but his conception of the one God has to be sufficiently inclusive to cover those Three Who, as he knows, certainly possess the attributes of Deity. The Mussulman on the other hand does not pretend to know anything about the attributes of Deity, excepting that God is one, invisible and omnipotent. Consequently he frames his definition of the Deity so as to purposely exclude what the Christian with his larger knowledge knows to be the manifestation of the same essence.

To pass on to the Mussulman's conception of his religion as it relates to the prophet. The *paighambarī*, or the bringing of messages from the Deity, is in many ways a peculiar idea. Mohammed himself had very little notion of his message being an advance on what had been given before, and of the gradual growth of revelation he had no conception at all. He was content to assert that his teaching was the religion of Abraham, a phrase of which he frequently made use. It is true that Mussulmans sometimes say that parts of God's Word were revealed to former *paighambars*, but that the complete commandment was given to Mohammed, and although this is very different from the Christian doctrine of the growth of revelation, it might possibly be regarded as a substitute for it; but the fact is that, though it may be traceable to the prophet, it is quite foreign to the essential system of Islam. We frequently find such foreign ideas which have been imported into Islam, occasionally by Mohammed but more frequently by his followers, simply to answer some specific objection, or to maintain the superiority of the system over all others. Such importations can as a rule be easily separated from the essential doctrines of Islam, and in most cases they have not affected the general character of the religion. This is due to the religion as first conceived by Mohammed having been clear in its essential points, and it is these points rather than the accretions that have left such a strong mark upon the body of Mussulmans. The *paighambari*, more than any other doctrine or expression of doctrine, brings out with intense plainness the fundamental distinction between the Mussulman and the Christian, that enormous divergence of view regarding the moral law which lies at the root of almost all their differences in subordinate theories and tenets. So when we are discussing the influence of Mohammedan ideas upon character, it is well to remember that sects which do not hold this theory of the *paighambari* ought to be regarded separately.

There are in Persia sects which are only nominally Mussulman, and which largely owe their origin to non-Mohammedan sources. The Sūfis, for instance, are only half Mohammedan, and their philosophy is really pantheistic. Sufis are to be found in Yezd, but there are not very many serious ones, and the sect has largely lost its direct influence in the country. But the Babis, of whom the Behāī branch is rapidly spreading everywhere throughout the Persian towns, have been influenced by Sufi ideas to a much greater extent than have the orthodox Shiahs, who, we agreed, are not pantheistic. Perhaps some professing Behāīs are really very near to the Sufis in ideas, but this is not the case with the more orthodox, who, though they have modified the fundamental doctrines of Mohammedanism in such a way as to remove the gulf between God and the prophet, have not produced a theology which is free from the obvious defects of that of Islam. The Behāī appears to hold that the superior prophet, that is, the book-bearer, is in every case an incarnation of the Deity, but he goes on to say that there is an absolute distinction between the prophet and his people; for the book-bearer is God, and the people are not God; nor are they, so far as I can understand, capable of receiving the Spirit of God, either from the prophet or directly from God Himself. They can only be impressed by the prophet as wax is impressed by a seal. Whether this doctrine is really Behāu'llah's or not, it was certainly given to me by men who ought to have known the truth about the Behāī faith.

The adherents of this sect in Persia are now exceedingly numerous, and many people believe that in the end the whole country will become Behāī;

so the question whether the Behāīs are more reliable than the orthodox Shiahs has become an important one. Certainly they teach a cleaner and purer doctrine on points of ethics; but what Persia needs is not so much a higher moral teaching, but rather a higher basis for morality. A religion that puts the commandment not to steal on the same level as the direction not to stew your dates but to fry them, will never produce the high characters that are to be found in such communities as the Parsi. It would be irreverent to compare such a faith with the religion given to us by the Saviour.

During the late Behāī massacre, I had the opportunity of discussing what was going on with a Behāī *muballigh*, that is, an authorised Behāī teacher and missionary. I have no intention of unnecessarily dwelling on the ghastly horrors that were then being perpetrated, but a few details are unavoidable. The Behāī sectaries were not at that time being executed before the *mujtahids*, but were being torn in pieces by the crowd. What had excited the people was not simply religious feeling, but it was very largely the statement by the clerical authorities that the goods of the Behāīs were "lawful," that is, that any one might plunder them who cared to do so. The attacks were often made by men who had lived for a long while in close companionship with the Behāīs, knowing them all the time to be members of the sect, and yet consorting and eating with them freely. Holes were bored in the heads of some of these poor wretches with awls, oil was then poured into the hole and lighted. Other forms of torture were used about which one cannot write. Women and children were very seldom actually killed, but were fearfully ill-treated, and sometimes left to die of starvation. It was reported that in one of the villages Babi children died within full sight of the villagers, after waiting for days under the trees where their murdered parents had left them.

The Behāī *muballigh* with whom I was talking was certainly well aware, in a general way, of what was going on; yet I could not get him to see that these things, done in the name of religion to his own sect, were in themselves wrong, and that man's eyes had been opened, or could be opened, to their essential wrongness. Of course he maintained that the action of the Mussulmans was evil, but his reason was that, in the first place, those persecuted were spiritually right, and, in the second place, even had they not been so, the last book-bearer, the Behāu'llah, had promulgated a Divine commandment that there was to be no religious persecution. I then asked him if such persecution could again become lawful if another book-bearer appeared and promulgated a different commandment. He answered that it was impossible for another book-bearer to appear for a long period. I then asked him if he would accept a new book-bearer, who, besides satisfying the other conditions, exhibited a text in one of the previously received

Scriptures, stating that one day in God's sight is as a thousand years. He replied that, if such a verse could be shown, and the other conditions were satisfied, such a man might be accepted to-morrow, even although he taught a doctrine similar to that of Mohammed about religious persecution and other matters of the same sort.

Now there are three points to be noted by those who expect great things of the Behāī movement. First of all, the Behāīs accept the whole of the Jewish and Christian Scriptures, which, of course, include a verse of the kind above mentioned. Secondly, they have already had three book-bearers; the Bab, who was the original founder of the Babi sects, and who not only exhibited a Divine book, but also claimed to be the resurrection of Mohammed in the same way that Mohammed was the resurrection of Jesus; Subhi Azal, whom for some years they recognised as the Bab's successor; and lastly, Behāu'llah, whom the Behāīs now hold to be the only major prophet of the three. Thirdly, the Behāīs, in attempting to prove that the Bab was a lesser prophet and a mere forerunner of the Behāu'llah, and also that Subhi Azal was never a really great personage, have seriously falsified their records. The reader who desires further information on this subject cannot do better than consult Professor E. G. Browne's admirable introduction to his translation of the *Tārīkhi Jadīd*.

The Bab, who came forward rather less than a century ago, was a young Shirazi Persian, a Seyid of the merchant class, whose real name was Ali Mohammed. The Shaikhi sect were at that time predicting the appearance of a great religious leader, and the Bab came forward claiming to be this prophet. He called himself the Bab, or Gate of Knowledge, and was at first supposed by his followers to be the Gate of Access to the Mehdi; but he seems to have used these terms in a very broad and allegorical fashion, and to have held the doctrine of the essential unity of all book-bearers. He later declared himself to be the Mehdi, and also to be the Gate of Access to One Whom God should manifest.

The movement caused a great deal of fighting in Persia, and though the Babis were acting on the defensive, there is very little doubt that they had harboured political designs. The Bab, however, differs from Mohammed in having been, so far as we can judge, primarily a religious reformer, and having done his best to make the movement as spiritual as possible. His followers were treated with the most barbarous severity, and he himself was after a few years put to death. Before this he appointed Subhi Azal, one of his followers, to be his successor, and for a few years this man was received as "He Whom God should manifest." Later on, Subhi Azal's half-brother, the Behāu'llah, managed to get himself accepted as head of the sect. Many of the followers of Subhi Azal were assassinated, and the sect was re-organised with some important differences. It now purports to be absolutely non-political, and the teaching has become more simple and practical. The Behāīs are anxious to retain the use of the *Quran*, so as to preserve their claim to toleration, although they imagine that the law of the *Quran* no longer stands, its place having been taken by a later revelation. Partially to avoid inconsistency in this matter, and partially to keep before the minds of the Mussulmans the possibility of one really divine book being replaced by another, they encourage the reading of all the Scripture considered divine by Mohammedans, that is, not only the *Quran*, but also the whole of the Christian Bible, nor do they generally call the authenticity of the extant version in question.

Behāīism is obviously an attempt to adapt Islam to the exigencies of modern circumstances, taking advantage of the special tenets of the Shiahs. The North of Persia is being at present rapidly overrun by Russia, and even in the South the Persian feels that he is on the eve of political changes. The Behāīs consider that they have a creed which enables them to meet the foreigner without continual jar and offence. In this they are right, for they do not veil their women, they do not consider infidels unclean, and they go further than does the broadest Shiah in the matter of respect to other forms of faith. Some orthodox Shiahs accept the Jewish and Christian Scriptures as they stand, without pressing the story that the Jews and Christians altered their books to suit their own purposes. Almost all Persians are open to argument on this point, though most will say that to those possessed of the *Quran* the perusal of former Scriptures is unnecessary. But the Behāīs hold that, unless started by a real prophet, no religion can possibly survive, and consequently they allow to even the grossest forms of idolatry a divine origin, and the possession of a certain substratum of truth.

In Persia there can never have been that almost impenetrable wall of dogmatic assertion and self-assurance which seems to exist in many Sunni lands, but something of the kind is to be found throughout Islam. As the self-satisfaction of the Behāī is almost as strong as that of the Sunni, and infinitely stronger than that of the Shiah, it seems a paradox to say that Babiism has given us in Persia a prepared soil for missionary work. The fact is that the field prepared is not amongst the Babis themselves, but amongst the Shiahs who have been in touch with Babis, and are nevertheless unconvinced. Consequently it is a field which cannot be expected to last for ever, but of which advantage ought to be taken immediately, for it is very seldom that we find so exceptional an opportunity given to us for attacking Mohammedanism on its own ground.

In Yezd the Behāīs have attached to themselves many of the most enlightened Mussulmans. The teaching of the sect about behaviour and practice is not bad, though, in matters connected with women, there is an inclination to adopt customs that are rather dangerous considering the low moral atmosphere. The tendency to minimise the miraculous element in religion is not altogether wholesome, and some professing Babis are inclined to a rather crude rationalism, the end of which it is difficult to foresee. This tendency is perhaps fostered by the peculiar manner of interpreting the sacred books, a method difficult to describe, as it fluctuates between the wildest flights of metaphor, and the lowest depths of puerile literalism, the balance between the two being decided by a very determined preconception of what ought to be. To give a specimen of this, it was seriously urged in a Behāī pamphlet, reviewed and summarised by the Rev. W. A. Rice in the *Church Missionary Intelligencer*, that Isaiah xxv. 6-9, where God is described as making "unto all people a feast of fat things, a feast of wine on the lees, of fat things full of marrow, of wines on the lees well refined," refers to the entertaining of visitors by Behāu'llah during his banishment at Acre. The "wines on the lees well refined" are the tea, which Persians generally pour through a small strainer. The passage also refers to the fact that God "will swallow up death in victory," and will "wipe away all tears from off all faces; and the rebuke of His people shall He take away from off all the earth." To this part only a spiritual interpretation is given.

I tried before I left Persia to find out the impression that the sect had made upon other Europeans, so as not to give a one-sided opinion about them. Personally, I came to the conclusion that, in matters even remotely connected with religion, they were less truthful than the ordinary Shiah, but that in the ordinary affairs of life they were a trifle more reliable. Some other missionaries had a lower opinion of their truthfulness, and most of those who had had business dealings with them considered that they were not more trustworthy than ordinary Mussulmans. My conclusion is that, though they may succeed in establishing their creed in Persia, and may even make the Persians more easy to deal with, they will not greatly alter the moral character of the people. They have not done so hitherto, and an examination of their faith shows that they cling, in the main, to the Mussulman theory of the *paighambari*, or at any rate have not changed it for a doctrine which gives a man more cogent reasons for adhering to an approved line of conduct in times of difficulty.

The name given in Mohammed's system to the state of the true believer is *Islām*, which means "Resignation to God." By this the Mussulman seems to understand that he must not criticise the prophet, whatever he may do or teach, and that in the same way he must accept everything that happens as the will of God. A waiving of personal responsibility, and an acceptance of all occurrences as the Divine intention, is to the Persian an undoubted virtue. The steadfast pursuit of a purpose which has been thwarted will often appear to him actually vicious, although such persistency might be justified in his eyes by its success, which would prove it to have been in harmony with God's will.

The word which expresses the duty of the believer being *Islam*, or resignation, the corresponding word used by the Mussulman to describe his theory of the course of events is *taqdīr*, or predestination. There is, as I have said, in Shiah dogma an attempt to modify the extreme predestinarian doctrines of the Sunni. But these doctrines are so much an integral part of Mohammedanism that it is impossible for the Mussulman, Shiah or otherwise, to be anything but a gross fatalist. This then completes the list of names under which the essential and fundamental conceptions of Islam are taught, *Tauhid, Paighambari, Islam*, and *Taqdir*.

There are also in Mohammedanism certain other doctrines which seem to be part of the system, but which are not quite so fundamental as those that have been stated. Some of these are not quite plain: it is very difficult, for instance, to understand what was Mohammed's teaching on the forgiveness of sins, and there is great confusion of thought on this point amongst his followers. Certainly an infidel becoming a Mussulman has his sins forgiven, though he does not expect to receive any peculiar strength for the future, but only a direction as to what God wants him to do and to avoid. After this the motives of his actions will be *khauf u jizā*, that is to say, the fear of Hell and the expectation of Heaven. He will have to be punished in Hell for his sins according to their assessed value, unless he has previously wiped them out, either by *savābs*, that is, by works of merit, or by repentance. Repentance of a real kind is supposed to have a certain value, though it is hard to state exactly what that value is. Formal repentance, which does not in the mind of the common Persian necessarily involve the giving up of such fruits of sin as stolen articles, has also a certain value. But the most efficient way of atoning for sin is by *savabs*. Finally no Mussulman, at any rate among the Shiahs, would consider it justifiable to hold himself free from the fear of Hell.

Punishment in Hell according to the Mussulman idea is not necessarily everlasting, for most of the Persians believe that, by the intercession of Mohammed, all his people will finally get to Heaven. But in Heaven there are many grades, and the position of the individual will be determined by the relative weight of his *savabs* and sins. Properly, a *savab* is a work of supererogation considered as possessing merit; but the word is often used less exactly for any action which will be put to the account of a man as a good deed. I believe that Persian Mohammedans when using this word almost universally accept the view that the performance of a certain number of approved actions makes it less necessary to adhere to the path of duty.

Also, to put it crudely, the good deed is not regarded as the gift of God to man, but as the gift of man to God; and I feel convinced that the word is bound up with the assumption that Heaven-seeking or the fear of Hell are the only possible motives for right behaviour.

The ordinary Yezdi has no doubt that a non-Mussulman can do a *savab*, especially if he benefits a Mussulman; and the belief that such a man if he was a Jew or a Christian, could get to Heaven, would not be considered very heretical.[4] Some Yezdis might allow that idolaters could get to Heaven by *savabs*, but this would be considered a more dangerous doctrine. The fact is that there was in Mohammed's essential teaching a very large amount of latitudinarianism, and this comes out in the common ideas of Mussulmans who are not repressed by a system such as that of the Sunnis.

The merit of an action is decided by the intention of the doer and not by its result. This is brought out by a native story, framed for the purpose.

"One day a traveller came to a well, where he dismounted, fastened his animal to a pin, and satisfied his thirst. As he returned to his animal it occurred to him that it would be a *savab* to leave the pin behind, for other travellers who might wish to tether their beasts. The next to arrive at the well was a man on foot, who, being very thirsty and in a hurry, fell over the pin. This man threw the pin down the well, so as to prevent any one else from having a similar accident. A learned man in the neighbourhood was asked which of the two did the *savab*, the man who left the pin or the man who threw it away. He answered, 'Both, for their intentions were equally good.'"

That there is truth in this teaching is obvious, but the story ignores the necessity of taking thought and pains, so that one's impulses may not do more harm than good. This is always ignored in Persia, and I think I am right in putting it down to the teaching connected with the use of the word. Large sums of money are given for the poor, and yet the alleviation of poverty is very small; and the same sort of thing happens in other branches of philanthropy. The gift once given, the donor loses all interest in its bestowal; funds are squandered on the most paltry objects, and the general effect seems to be that money given in this way becomes money wasted. Charity is also much vitiated in Persia by unpractical, and in many cases superstitious ideas. To give alms to a Seyid is a greater *savab* than to help an ordinary beggar, so a large proportion of the philanthropy of Persia goes to support a begging class, who are in every way a burden, and in some ways a danger to society. The Seyids are also more lightly punished, and consider themselves outside the reach of the very small amount of justice that exists. Again, it is more meritorious to give on a Thursday, as the eve of the Friday holiday, or on the eve of a feast, than on an ordinary day; and lastly, the people expect that they will amass more merit by giving microscopic sums to all comers than by giving more effective assistance to a limited number.

As I have said, the doctrine connected with *savabs* acknowledges only two motives of action, the fear of punishment and the expectation of reward, and it is not allowed that any other motive can possibly exist. Persian women are very inquisitive, and one day some of them were questioning the ladies of the Yezd mission as to what they ate for breakfast. When it transpired that the others ate eggs and one did not, the remark was immediately made, "You see she is trying to get a higher place in Heaven." At another time when my wife was trying to explain to some women that we do not look to works of merit to secure salvation, she was met by the answer, "But the *Hakīm Khānum* (lady doctor) does; or why should she have taken all that trouble about the Seyid's wife when she was ill?"

Shiahs often consider that by letting others do a *savab* for them they confer a favour greater than they themselves receive. One might imagine that this would only apply to benefactors who agreed with their religious notions; but even if you can convince a Shiah that you do not believe in the possibility of winning Heaven by *savabs*, he will reply, very logically, that your want of faith does not prevent the fact being true, and that it is absurd to expect him to be grateful because of your unbelief in facts. I remember trying to make a very badly-behaved youngster, who was in the school under my charge, see that we had some reason to expect more gratitude from him, as we had really taken great trouble with him, and Christians did not think it necessary to do such things for the sake of their future welfare. His answer was that if we did not consider that *savabs* were necessary Mussulmans did.

Savabs are not necessarily good actions, but almost all actions which are directly kind are included in the term. So although the doctrine connected with *savabs* is not in every way a good thing, it still has a certain value. Of course it is true that men who are anxious to do big *savabs* in order to wipe off the sins of very evil lives generally choose non-ethical ones. During the late Babi massacre a soldier found a Yezdi who was dragging about another man, and trying to make out whether he was really a Behāī. "You see," he said, "I have been a wicked man all my life, and have never said my prayers or done any other *savabs*, so, unless I can do a big *savab*, I shall certainly go to Hell. If this man is a Babi, I mustn't let him go, for if I kill an infidel of course I shall go straight to Heaven." Nevertheless the ordinary *savab* is a kind action, and in the idea of their efficacy we get something almost corresponding to a moral principle. Sometimes indeed the Persian's conception of a work of merit tends to correct and check the worse commandments of his code. For instance, although the killing of a Babi as an infidel may be considered a *savab*, the saving of a life, even if it is the life of the same Babi, may also be held a meritorious act of a different kind.

That the Persian's notions as to what constitutes an act of merit are a saving clause in his religion I have no doubt at all. I am, however, not quite certain whether this saving clause properly belongs to Mohammedanism, for it bears on the face of it a family likeness to the doctrines of superior systems, and it will not quite fit into the system of Islam. The rest of the Shiah ideas about Heaven, Hell, the efficacy of *savabs*, and repentance, seem to be really Mussulman, though everything is not quite coherent. Perhaps the fact is that in these points Mohammed was an opportunist, and taught any doctrine which he thought would make people obedient to his law. He was careful not to expect too much, and, while keeping his followers as long as possible in a state of uncertainty as to their salvation, he tried never to shut the door on hope. So it is questionable whether either the teaching of the Quran, or the ideas of the Persians on these subjects, could possibly be presented in a quite consistent form.

I have tried to enumerate in this chapter just those doctrines which form the original philosophy or theology upon which everything in Islam rests, and to show that not only does the ordinary Shiah Yezdi accept them *in toto*, but that, with the one small exception that has been stated, all his fundamental beliefs are to be found in this category. Of course these ideas are a much more serious part of a religion than is a code of commandments that is not believed to be permanent. Indeed it is quite possible that greater laxity in the observance of such a code may be due to a juster appreciation of the notions with which it was promulgated. To say that Persia has not been greatly influenced by Mohammedanism because the Persians get drunk in their houses, is shallow criticism. It is still shallower to imagine that the fact that some of the Shiah ordinances are in themselves laxer than the Sunni makes it plain that Persians are less Mussulman than Turks and Indians.

For instance, the Shiahs have a custom of temporary marriages, according to which it is lawful for a man, besides the four regular wives allowed by Islam, to have as many inferior wives as he likes, contracting these marriages for any length of time he pleases, from a few days upwards. There is, however, a legal fiction by which these women are supposed to be lowered to the rank of slaves, which ought to entirely remove the Sunni objection; for, unless it can be proved that the temporary ownership of a slave is impossible, it is very difficult to understand why this evasion should not be considered quite legitimate according to the undoubted principles of

Mohammedanism. That there is a certain amount of latitudinarianism in Shiah Islam is indisputable, but so there is in the whole of Mohammed's teaching and practice.

As a matter of fact his attitude towards Jews and Christians, and even towards the idolaters, was largely opportunist. At one time he made leagues with the Jews, promising that they should not be disturbed in their religion; at other times he picked quarrels with them, and put every one who would not accept Islam to the sword. This latitudinarianism has found its way into the Quran itself, where a verse is to be found telling Mohammedans that they may eat the food of "the people of the book," that is, of the people holding religions whose origin he recognised as divine. The strict Shiahs in Yezd interpret this as meaning dry food. They make a great distinction between wet and dry; only a few years ago it was dangerous for an Armenian Christian to leave his suburb and go into the bazaars in Isfahan on a wet day. "A wet dog is worse than a dry dog." Nevertheless, there are great differences of opinion on this point, and most non-clerical Shiahs would take tea at any European's house. There was a Shiah woman who used to freely take tea at the house of a Christian lady, the lady herself making it and pouring it out, but she refused to use the tea-glasses used in the same house by Babi women. Another Shiah lent a donkey for a Christian lady, but told her that he could not use it again if she allowed her Parsi nurse to ride upon it. And yet it is more easy to get the Mussulmans to eat food with the Parsis than with the Jews, whose religion ranks higher than Zoroastrianism in the popular regard, though they themselves are specially despised by the Mohammedans. This curious mixture of breadth and bigotry is only explicable on the assumption that the Shiah's main ideal is exactly that opportunist position which was taken up by Mohammed during his lifetime.

Perhaps we ought not to leave this subject without discussing rather more fully the assertion which has been made about the Persian Shiahs, that they have changed the doctrine of the unity of God for a loose pantheism, and have dethroned the Quran for the utterance of Sufi poets. That the Persians as a race have an extreme veneration for Sufi poetry, which contains expressions of questionable orthodoxy, cannot well be called in question; but before discussing the more serious part of the allegation, it is necessary to thoroughly understand about whom it is stated; for there are small Shiah sects, of whom it is quite true that they are only half Mussulman, but these are very different from the sect which is at present predominant in Persia, and which in Yezd at any rate does not appear to lack veneration for the Quran. One point, however, must be granted, and that is, that all Persian Mussulmans, orthodox or otherwise, are often led to express acquiescence in a statement which appears to be in itself correct, however opposed it may be to the general tenor of their other beliefs. The fact is that they do not easily see a contradiction, and this has made it possible for the Shiah to accept poetry which he would otherwise have absolutely rejected. I do not myself know a single Christian doctrine to which I could not get most Shiahs to agree, if I was careful to state it in language with which they were familiar, and not to dwell on its divergence from the Mussulman idea.

But doctrines so allowed to pass, whether Christian or Sufi, would have no strength against the system of Islam, which most Yezdis have grasped as an integral whole. The general plan of Mussulman doctrine, constructed as it was for inhabitants of a desert, is peculiarly comprehensible to people like the Yezdis, who are accustomed to isolated objects and ideas, and are slow at grasping a too elaborately connected argument. For the system of Islam is not elaborately connected: that there is a general consistency in it, is true, but the consistency is like that of a certain housewife's accounts, in which a large number of items were entered under the heading of "forgets." The accounts were true and accurate, but they were not highly instructive. Similarly in Islam a large variety of commandments have been labelled, "commandments for the age of Moses," or "commandments for the age of Mohammed," and the doctrine of the *paighambari* is so formulated as to make further systematisation unnecessary. This being a scheme of arrangement which a Persian can understand, it has laid hold of his mind to a peculiar degree. Phrases and expressions that are opposed to it, he will often accept, but their influence on his behaviour is exceedingly small. The thing which dominates him, and will, unless explicitly resisted and combated, always continue to dominate him, is Islam and Islam alone.

Before going on to discuss in another chapter some other important aspects of the Yezdi's religion, it will be well to consider how the whole Mussulman theory has affected his character. First of all, it has made him even more disposed to unconnected and disjunctive views of life than he would otherwise have been. This becomes plain when we compare him with his fellow-townsmen who have been in touch with other religions. Secondly, we find that he possesses a very low view of the value of morality, which in Mohammedanism has no unique place, but is only one of the ways of attaining salvation. Another way is through accuracy of religious observance, and, when a Persian takes to this, he generally abandons any attempt to live straight. Residents in the country are well aware of this, and are justly inclined to distrust a man who is very particular about his prayers and ceremonial duties.

I must ask the reader to pardon me if I have said in this chapter anything which appears disrespectful to Mohammedanism. In trying to record facts and to correctly weigh impressions, one cannot avoid frankly stating what has been forcibly brought before both mind and eyes, even though the things stated may not be exactly what they are expected to be. The fact is that Islam has ruined Persia; and it is not fair to the real character of the people to underrate the effect that this religion has produced on them. As to Mohammed, I believe that I have stated nothing about him which is not a matter of common knowledge. Doubtless the author who starts with the determination to write an interesting and sympathetic book, will be able, by selecting his incidents, to convey a more favourable impression, just as a criminal lawyer may be able to find much in favour of even a guilty client; but the historical critic who starts on the examination of Mohammed's history without any pre-judgment must necessarily find it difficult not to come to a very unfavourable conclusion. The Arabian prophet headed a monotheistic movement which had started without him, and which would have probably succeeded to a very large extent whether he had touched it or not, and to this movement he did a great deal of damage without making any serious ethical contribution. It may be readily admitted that Mohammed was an attractive person, and that he possessed other great gifts, one of which was unusual eloquence. He seems to have been an enthusiast who in his worst moments absolutely believed in himself and in his mission, and there is no doubt that he drew into his company, both by persuasion and violence, men who might have looked askance at a more spiritual leader. But those who want to know what Islam does for a people who accept it had better compare the Yezdi Mussulman with the Yezdi Parsi. The Parsis have a curious and interesting religion, the main point of which seems to be the belief that God has created all things of the four elements, and that He therefore expects from all His creatures a reverential and sympathetic treatment of one another. The religion is Gospelless, it is coated over with gross superstitions, and it has the very great defect of being so elementary in its teaching that there is a strong tendency amongst its professors to deny revelation altogether, and to become simply rationalists. For all this the Zoroastrian Parsi possesses, as a rule, a strong moral character, which, when he becomes a Mohammedan, is almost always lost in a few generations. Unfortunately, the Behāī movement is just now attracting a large number of Zoroastrians, and is becoming a serious danger; for the Behāī, whatever he may say to the contrary, is really a Mussulman, and his system, in which opportunism takes the place of the doctrine of the growth of the moral law, retains most of the more serious defects of Islam. However, as the majority of the Yezdi Parsis are not likely to become Behāīs, it is a matter for congratulation that any European power that may have to solve the problem of establishing good government in Southern Persia will find ready to hand a considerable community of this intelligent and interesting people in at least one of the Persian towns.

CHAPTER IV

It is now necessary for us to touch on some aspects of Mohammedanism in Yezd with which it was impossible to deal fully while sketching the essential system. In the last chapter we were primarily dealing with the religious ideas that had been brought to bear upon the country as influences, but in this chapter we shall speak rather more of their results. First of all, I should like to give two stories. I give the two, because one is the account of a conversation which I had with a man who was not an orthodox Shiah; and, although I fancy I have heard similar remarks made by men whose orthodoxy was unimpeachable, it is well to be on the safe side. I had been challenged to give my reasons for preferring Christianity to Mohammedanism, and in reply I gave an account of a conversation I had had with another Mohammedan only a day or two before. I had been trying to show him that lying was a sin, and he had replied to me: "It's all very well for Ferangis to say that; but the fact is that they can't tell lies, and we can." I quoted this story simply as bringing out very forcibly a common Persian idea, for Persians trust Ferangis implicitly, not because they respect them, but because they believe they have a constitutional difficulty in telling lies. Having quoted it, I went on to say that as we all acknowledged in theory that truth-telling was right, it was reasonable to infer that a religion which had produced a mental constitution supposed to be incapable of falsehood, was better than a religion which had produced the exact contrary. The answer of the Mohammedan was that truth-speaking and honesty had nothing to do with religion, but were purely a matter of climate. "In that case," I said, "the people of Persia ought to speak the truth very well, for one of the Greek historians who lived before the Mohammedan era declared that the Persians were famous for speaking the truth." "But who does not know," said the Mohammedan, "that the climate of a country changes entirely every two thousand years?"

At another time a Mohammedan of undoubted orthodoxy was answering a similar position, only he was trying to explain away not only the difference in honesty, but also in other matters. He said: "These facts cannot be denied, but they prove the truth of Islam, and not its falsity. If you find that thieves have broken the doors and windows of a house, do you not conclude that there is something worth stealing inside?" I have reason to believe that this is a well-known retort, for other Europeans in other parts of Persia have been met by it. It is therefore well worth examination. I myself find in it two assumptions which seem to me to be peculiar features of Islam. First there is the assumption that the possession of the treasure gives no safety to the doors and windows: that is to say that the possession of true religion does not in any way assist the keeping of God's commandments. The fact is that Mohammed's commandment is not expected to be a source of spiritual strength, but only a set of orders. Then there is the equally un-Christian assumption that the keeping of the moral commandments of God is in no sense the treasure, but something entirely extraneous to it, which is not essential to the state of the treasure-holder. These two assumptions are to be found running through the whole of Persian Islam, and producing the most extraordinary results. Very few Mohammedans will hesitate to acknowledge the low state of Mussulman morality as opposed to that of the Armenians, or even of the Parsis, whom they regard as little better than idolaters. If a Mussulman of the teacher class has anything to gain by confessing or making it plain to an infidel that he has been guilty of gross sin, he will not consider that he has in the least forfeited his claim to a superior position by doing so.

Of course being non-ethical the religion becomes superstitious. The Mohammedan considers that there is no known principle by which the commands of the Deity can be connected and understood, consequently he admits actions in his religious code which we should regard as ridiculous. The whole theory of Mussulman pilgrimages is absurd, and the practice is even more so. What can be more intrinsically foolish, as well as heartless and cruel, than the custom of sending off the old women, when they are past work, to some holy shrine, under the impression that, if they die on the very difficult journey, as in a certain class of cases they generally do, they will go straight to Heaven? It is rather a ghastly custom to send vast quantities of bodies for interment in the exceedingly inadequate space at Qum, over a country where there is no vehicular transport. But the natural demand for a more easy set of roads to Heaven has caused a multiplication of such practices as these far beyond anything that was originally taught in the mosques. Things have gone so far in this respect, that the most popular edition of the Quran in Persia is a very minute round one in two parts, absolutely illegible, and only suitable for wearing in a sewn-up case.

As in most superstitious countries, we find a number of superstitions connected with divining; and these are largely sanctioned by the mullas, who will divine with the Quran in a mosque for a fee. The commoner form of divining is with a rosary, rather on the plan of "Two, four, six, eight, Mary at the cottage gate." Persians use this to an extent that is hardly believable. They will consult the beads as to whether to send for the doctor, and again, after he has come, to see whether they should buy the medicine he prescribes, and finally, after buying it, they consult them once more before deciding whether the patient shall take a dose. At the same time it is quite permissible to "call threes." A woman with raging toothache got permission from the beads to send for a European lady to extract the tooth, but on taking the beads for the extraction after her arrival they were unfavourable, so arrangements were at once made for divining with the Quran at a mosque, which would of course overrule any result with the beads. A Persian will consider himself quite justified in breaking a business engagement if the beads tell him he had better avoid the interview; indeed very often he will not so much as fix a date for the payment of a bill before he has consulted his almanac, and discovered which are the lucky and which are the unlucky days.

CORPSES EN ROUTE TO THE QUM CEMETERY.

SANDY DESERT NEAR YEZD.

The vast empty deserts which surround Yezd, and the huge mountain ridges which form the horizon are to the Yezdi by no means empty. It is an axiom of science that Nature abhors a vacuum, and it is a corresponding psychological law that the human imagination cannot tolerate absolute emptiness. So the Yezdi, like the Arabian, peoples his deserts with *jins* and *dīvs* and devils, and wherever there is a space not filled in he imagines strange forms of animal life. At the risk of being considered superstitious myself I must own that I should like to see some of the travellers' tales of Persia more carefully investigated, particularly those relating to the existence of very large lizards which are dangerous to human life. One is familiar with the defences that are being constantly brought forward for the fable of the sea-serpent; how that the sea is after all an almost unknown waste, only crossed in a very few places by well established water-roads that can be most easily avoided; and although the desert cannot be said to afford as much cover as the ocean, for it is not possible to plunge below the surface at any point at any time, still its vast expanses are almost as untraversed and unknown as the ocean wastes, and there are not a few places, especially in the mountains, honeycombed with caves and clefts. This however is a digression. In such a country as I have described, with its vast and barren solitudes, it would be difficult for a people to exist and maintain their reason, if they did not believe in something corresponding to the *jins* and *divs*. Consequently we find *jins* in the keyholes, *jins* in the *qan'ats*, *divs* in the mountains, *divs* in the rocks, anywhere, everywhere, a vast population filling up the huge interstices left by Nature. Most of this population is malevolent; so naturally the ordinary Persian is a mass of charms: nobody goes about without cold iron in his pocket, and a large number of people wear either the sacred book in its entirety, or large portions of it somewhere about their person. Also they are terribly afraid of the evil eye; and numbers of their charms, especially for the children, are directed against it. It is not that they think the evil eye common: any Persian will tell you that very few people have it, but they all know of at least one case, and they are terribly afraid of it, sometimes refusing to admit strangers to their house until they are satisfied they have not got it. If a mother sees a dead body before the birth of her child, then, unless she takes the precaution of placing some salt on the corpse, and afterwards putting a little of it in the child's eye, her child will inevitably have the evil eye, and everything that is pleasing to its eye will be cursed. The evil eye is likely to kill children of tender years, so very young children are always hidden under the *chādar* when carried in the street.

These superstitions are exceedingly general, and sometimes co-exist with a certain amount of intelligence and education. I remember a man who had obviously been in touch with some of the Persian mystics, and was quite capable of discussing and more or less understanding complicated ideas, telling me that he considered that the silkworm owners in the Yezd district were exceedingly wise in refusing to admit strangers to see the worms. He explained to me that they were creatures of such extreme harmlessness and guilelessness that they were peculiarly susceptible to malevolent influences from the outside world.

Superstitions of this kind will be found in all countries, and in most lands there are in addition superstitions that seem to be more intimately connected with the religion. The nature of the country fosters the tendency in Persia, and the Parsis are nearly as superstitious as the Mussulmans. But in Mohammedanism the peculiar difficulty is that there is nothing to guide a man in separating the superstitious practices from any connected with a central true idea. The whole religion is a medley of trivialities. The history of Mohammed and his early admiration for the Jews, with whom he must have been constantly in touch, explains this. He saw the result of their ceremonial law and their national religious customs, binding them together and making them a peculiar people in every action of their household life; but of the parabolic significance of this law, of the doctrinal system which governed it, he saw and was taught very little or nothing. Nor did he want it: he wanted simply the political result, and in getting this he was eminently successful. He copied the system, but he gave to Islam a maximum of ordinances containing a minimum of teaching. After his death the minutiæ went on accumulating, until everything in the life of a Mussulman took a religious colour. In Persia the very dress is supposed to be more or less modelled on that worn by the prophet. The people not only kill their animals and eat their food according to the precepts of the Quran, but relying on their very extensive traditions they follow a prescribed religious practice in attitude and language. Shiahs are particularly scrupulous about certain of their washings, and think almost as much about them as they do about the regularity of their prayers. "If I become a Christian, when and how am I to wash myself?" This is one of the commonest questions for an enquirer to put to a missionary. Another very common one is, "How am I to dress?" The Mussulman hardly understands you if you tell him that such points are left to the individual judgment. I remember a Persian trying to prove to me that I could not possibly consider all meats lawful and ceremonially clean, or I should eat cat. It is very difficult to explain to the Yezdi that the drinking of wine at meals is not a necessary Christian institution, and for this reason the consideration of the necessity of maintaining Christian liberty is in Persia rather an argument for total abstinence than against it. In Yezd we are continually being asked whether the commonest peculiarities of European custom, such as eating with a knife and fork, were ordained by Christ. In one house they had to make away with some kittens, and the servant was directed to dig a hole in the compound for their reception. While he was doing so he asked his mistress, "Did your prophet direct you to bury kittens?" But the extreme point of triviality was reached by a man who had seemed a most intelligent enquirer, and had asked me to explain the essential points of Christianity, to which he listened most attentively, appearing to weigh them in his mind. When I had finished, he paused to consider the whole position: "*Sahib*," he said very slowly, "*man mas'ala dāram.*" — "Sir, I have a religious question to bring before you." I said, "*Bifarmāyīd.*" — "Please proceed." "*Āyā Masīh,*" he said very deliberately, "*āvāz i sūtrā halāl dānist?*" — "Did Christ consider humming lawful?" I reassured him on the point, and tried to explain the spiritual nature of Christ's teaching. I then left the room to get a book, and, when I came back, he was humming to himself contentedly.

Religion also provides the Yezdi with his entertainments and excitements; the place of the theatre is taken by the Muharram miracle play, and that of the ordinary concert by the *rūza khānī* or religious recitation, while even street rioting is generally connected with the persecution of people who do not agree with the religious opinions of the rioters. All this serves to strengthen the attachment of the common people to the religious system, which stands to them in the place of country, standard of etiquette, habits of life and code of cleanliness. As a matter of fact religion is not quite the right term for the Mohammedan system, for religion means restraint, and the object of almost all of the other systems called religions has been to present a predominant idea which is to govern and restrain all other ideas and aspects of life. In Mohammedanism there is the predominant idea of the *tauhid* and *paighambari*, but this conception more resembles the central doctrine of a philosophy than the governing principle of a religion. To put it in other words, Mohammed sought by his theological teaching rather to include everything than to control everything. Consequently the Mussulman, who reflects the spirit of his master much more than is generally allowed, is never satisfied with himself unless he is using religious language. What he does matters comparatively little, but the way in which he regards his action matters a great deal. If he forgets to mention God's name, he corrects himself; but to his mind there is little or no blasphemy in connecting God's name with any action of life, important or trivial, good or bad. The result of this is that those who are accustomed to religions possessing more influence over moral action are amazed at the religiosity of the Mohammedan: but although this religiosity is a fact, the whole wonder of it ceases when the religion is carefully examined. Others are equally astounded at what they consider the hypocrisy of the Mussulman; but this also is a misnomer: a Mussulman is not hypocritical: rather he has taken up a position towards affairs which renders hypocrisy unnecessary.

In Persia, at any rate, there is a further mistake which ought to be guarded against. Islam is not mere worldliness sanctified by the use of religious terms: it includes a great deal of unworldly thought, although it combines all considerations, worldly or unworldly, with little if any distinction. Still it must be owned that the worldly considerations are apt to predominate, for the Persian Shiah seems to be a reflection of Mohammed, who suggested that pilgrimages should be used for purposes of trade, invited people to become Mussulmans for political reasons, and not only winked at the making of converts by threats and terrorism, but laid this down as one of the essential means for spreading the religion. It is not sufficient to call such a system politico-religious, for it not only includes matters of public expediency in the religious idea, but it also sanctifies considerations of expediency that are purely personal. Yet there is one thing that the missionary in such a land as Persia cannot too fully realise; and that is that he is dealing with people who are not in the least ashamed of doubleness of motive. In their view, two purposes are better than one; and when it has been proved that their purposes are worldly, it has still to be considered whether there is not an unworldly purpose as well.

Men frequently come to enquire about Christianity, drawn by what seems to us a strange mixture of motives. They naturally enough put their more spiritual purposes first, for they realise that these are most appreciated by those to whom they talk, and they also consider that things like this ought to have a theoretical priority. Temporal needs are, however, much more pressing, and these have just as much claim to be satisfied by a new religion. Of course such a position is likely to be fruitful, not only of the gravest difficulties, but also of the most lamentable misunderstandings.

It will be readily understood that a system like this can easily be made to cover ideas which appear inconsistent, and as a matter of fact, it is very difficult to define some of the notions which Persian Shiahs hold to a point of fanaticism. For instance, there is room for considerable difference of opinion as to how far the Yezdi regards the foreigner as unclean. The Mohammedan is taught to regard as unclean the eating of certain kinds of food, contact with certain animals, and also contact with the persons of people who have not been ceremonially cleansed. There seem, however, to be degrees of uncleanness. Mohammed in one verse of the Quran declared the food of the Christians and Jews, as well as all food that had been properly prepared by a Mussulman, to be lawful; but we cannot suppose that he regarded these different classes of food as equally clean. Bigoted Persians sometimes ignore this permission of their prophet's, and declare that it refers only to dry food prepared by Jews or Christians; but in this they are not consistent, for they eat dry food prepared by pagans also.

The truth is that the attitude of the Persian towards the infidel is not altogether decided by Mohammed's direct teaching, but to a very large extent it is based upon an elementary human feeling which can be found in almost every country under the sun. Most people in England have a physical shrinking from undue contact with other persons. We do not care to drink out of a cup that other people have used, until it has been washed; we should, very few of us, care to take alternate bites at an apple with somebody else, and most Englishmen have a very similar objection to kissing. We are much less particular about contact with the hand, though here also we feel that a line has got to be drawn somewhere. Within the family we are less particular. Of course in connection with these things there is in England a great deal of talk about infection and the laws of hygiene, but the instinct exists apart from any notion of hygiene at all. Now in Persia you have got to remember that everything takes a religious colour, and this has tended to slightly modify the natural instinct, breaking down the wall of reserve within the boundaries of Islam, and giving the feeling the colour of a religious prejudice when applied to the outside world. Of course there are hundreds of Yezdi Mussulmans who will eat freely with a European without the slightest scruple, and a still larger number who do not allow their scruples to make any practical difference: at the same time people who wish to get into close touch with the natives should remember that the feeling of *nijāsat*, or ceremonial uncleanness, is a somewhat complex one, and that it will be more easy to overcome it if a certain discretion is observed. Persians eating the food of a European are on the look out for anything which is strange and peculiar, and if such peculiarities are observed they naturally feel more strongly the difference between themselves and their host. This not only renders them less approachable, but it also makes them much more shy of adopting Christian ideas, and in the case of enquirers, who, as I have said before, find it very difficult to understand that our customs are not all regulated by religion, a feeling may grow up that the state of Christianity is not possible to a native Persian.

As this book is not about Mohammedanism but about the Yezdi, I have perhaps devoted as much space to the religion of Islam in Yezd as is warranted by my choice of subject matter. At the same time there is no doubt that I have left out a great deal that might have been said, even without going into those details of doctrine and practice which it has been my intention to avoid. I have tried to give some idea of what Islam means to ordinary people in an ordinary Persian town, and I have had to dwell rather more at length on points where there was danger of misconception either through too precise a study of the accurate doctrines of Islam, or through a too superficial view of the result. In doing this I fear that I may have passed over too rapidly the more familiar aspects of the religion, the intense excitement of the spectators and actors at the Muharram games, the mourning for Hasan and Husain, the frenzied fanaticism of the mob after a rousing sermon at the mosques, and the close adherence of many Mussulmans to washing and prayers. This is one side of Shiah Islam, but as it is better known I have attempted to give the other. I cannot, however, leave the subject without reminding those who have to do with Persians of two most important things; first, that there is a real spiritual seeking amongst Mussulmans, and that the presence of worldly motives does not preclude it; secondly, that there is real enthusiasm for their religion in spite of latitudinarian ideas. To the Mussulman, as has been before stated, the system of Islam is everything, and he clings to it as dearly as to life itself, for it represents to him every habit that he has formed, and its cause is the cause of every motive that he acknowledges to be possible.

The religious ceremonies which in Persia arouse the greatest enthusiasm and fervour are essentially Shiah. The yearly miracle play in the month of Muharram depicts the death of the Imam Husain, son of Ali and Fātima, and grandson of Mohammed. This is the occasion of the most violent exhibitions of emotion on the part of both players and spectators. Men lash their naked bodies with chains in an ecstasy of frenzy, and the whole crowd bursts into groans and tears of grief. Feeling runs so high, and becomes so unmanageable on these occasions, that the secular authorities have tried to keep the performances out of the larger towns. But the atmosphere which is created is not by any means anti-foreign in a general sense. The Imam

Husain was done to death by his co-religionists, and tradition reports that a Ferangi ambassador interceded with Yazīd for the martyr's life. This ambassador appears in the play, and Persians often try to borrow an English saddle for his horse from the European residents. At the performance at the big village of Taft, which is near Yezd, I think the ambassador was often dressed as a modern Englishman, but I cannot vouch for this. At Yezd itself, the miracle play was not acted; but the carrying of the Nakhl, a ceremony supposed to be fraught with the same kind of danger, took place yearly. The Nakhl is a huge wooden erection hung on one side with daggers, and on the other side with looking-glasses. There are several Nakhls in Yezd, and two are very large. This custom also is connected with the death of the Shiah martyrs. The Nakhl is supposed to be moved from its place in the square by the miraculous agency of Fatima; but a good many people take it on themselves to assist her. Lastly, there is a night set apart for the burning of Omar, the usurping Khalif, and the carrying of the effigy through the town is the occasion of extreme excitement. One cannot help being strongly reminded of Guy Fawkes' day in England. Omar, it must be remembered, is a Sunni saint.

CARRYING THE NAKHL IN THE BIG SQUARE IN YEZD.

CHAPTER V

If it were not absolutely essential to the purpose of a book like this that there should be a more or less detailed analysis of the character of the Yezdi, I should certainly shirk making such an analysis. The Yezdi's faults are numerous, glaring, and interesting. His virtues are not only fewer, but there is much less to be said about them. In the concrete man, these virtues show fairly prominently, the vices have their peculiar humour, and the whole is not unlovable. On paper, while discussing the different points of the Yezdi's character one by one, it will be almost impossible to convey the general effect made by the entire human being.

When one first becomes acquainted with the Yezdi, one is inclined to regard him as so inconsistent in matters of morals as to be utterly devoid of all principle, bad or good. There is the same uncertainty about his actions that there is about the fall of an unloaded die. But just as the fall of the die is regulated by the law of averages, so the actions of the Yezdi are more or less consciously decided by what can only be termed systematised inconsistency, a kind of law of balance which seems to him to possess the merit of a principle. When he has done a certain number of good actions, which it must be confessed is frequently the case, then it is time for him to do some bad ones; and *vice versâ*, when he has done enough bad ones, he comes back for a time to good ones. This is partially the result of the theory of *savabs*; and the painful thing about it is that it makes moral trustworthiness impossible. If a man holds this pernicious theory as it was sketched in a previous chapter, then the more he has done right in the past the more he will feel justified in doing wrong in the future; and this in Yezd is no mere nightmare, but the literal fact. A good many of the Yezdis are frequently fair and straight in their dealings, but I do not know a single Mussulman among them, with regard to whom it would be fairly safe to depend on his doing the right thing on any particular occasion simply because he knew it to be right. There are men whose ordinary habits are fairly good, but to a man who considers that derelictions of duty can be absolutely paid for by past or future acts of merit not necessarily involving very much trouble, the temptation to yield to slightly increased pressure is very strong, and is likely to frequently overcome the bias of habit.

On the other hand, Persians have very strong notions of loyalty both to causes and to individuals. Nothing has brought this out more than the history of the Babi movement, which has certainly exhibited the strength of Persian character. Boys and young men have in this movement willingly undergone the most terrible tortures in the service of their spiritual teachers and the common cause. It ought to be understood that the motives of the Babi martyr are not quite the same as those which have generally influenced the Christians who have died for their faith. The Christian martyrs have generally died rather than do some act which they felt to be sinful, or leave undone something which they regarded as essential. A large number of the Babi martyrs on the other hand have died because they chose not to deny their faith, which according to their tenets was perfectly permissible to do. Now I know of at least one man, a Persian of high position, who was killed as a Babi, but who would have preferred embracing Christianity. What was his connection with Babiism I cannot say: he would, I believe, have embraced Christianity had it not been that he shrank from a religion where a direct denial of one's faith must always be accounted sinful. Whatever he was, he certainly did not shrink from making his divergence from orthodox Islam dangerously plain, and in this way he met his death. My purpose in mentioning the fact is to show that it is most difficult to induce a Mussulman to accept a very hard and fast line. Of course the story is only an illustration and does not prove the point, because there must have been other considerations which made Babiism, or a degree of unorthodoxy which passed for Babiism, easier to such a man than Christianity. It is not necessary to suppose that he was only influenced by a dislike to unbending rules; for the inability to ever deny his faith might have exposed him to petty insults, which would have been to him worse than death. Also his position as a Christian would have been, humanly speaking, a more solitary one. Still, when all has been said, I am convinced that the constitutional dislike to a hard and fast rule played at least some part in bringing the man to his decision, and also that this dislike is more pronounced in the Mussulman Yezdi than in the Yezdi Parsi.

A Persian who attaches himself to an individual will often prove himself very trustworthy in all matters affecting that individual's interest; and generally speaking, attachment to a European would be likely to produce a more dependable loyalty than attachment to another Persian. The feeling that a European friend would always himself act in a certain manner frequently leads a Persian to try and act in the same way towards him. I remember a Persian servant once replying to my wife, who had expostulated with him on the subject of some egregious falsehood that he had just told in the bazaars, "Of course, Khanum, I don't tell lies to you, for you don't like it; but these people expect me to lie, and one couldn't tell the truth to them."

Perhaps one might go further, and say that the Yezdi Mussulman frequently questions the virtue of keeping to an abstract principle, particularly when by abandoning it one might do a good turn to a friend. Impartiality is a thing which he absolutely fails to understand: indeed he considers it simply another name for disloyalty, and here it is probable that most other Easterns would agree with him.

It is impossible to treat the inconsistency of Yezdi Mussulmans as simple weakness. It is rather the absence of such principles as Westerns generally possess than the inability to keep to them; and indeed it is often the result of other principles of a peculiar kind, diametrically opposed to those to which we are accustomed. The Yezdis are a free-handed folk, and they despise a man who does not spend freely. They like to appear to live up to their incomes, and I think that some of them have a feeling of the same kind about their debit and credit account with their Creator. Also we must not forget that Persian inconsistency is not always a deviation towards wrong, but equally often a deviation towards right. Though in Persia it is never well to trust to a man's character, it is always advisable to appeal to high principles, even when dealing with apparently the most abandoned. While we were in Yezd we were brought into contact with three men in high position, whose names it is not necessary to mention, but whom I would put down as the three worst prominent men in Yezd. The first was an aristocratic official, the second a cleric, and the third an official and a *nouveau riche*. Now each of these three at some time or other made himself conspicuous by conduct that one was bound to commend and approve. It is impossible to always analyse motives, but in at least one case the action seemed to have been due to nothing but a disinterested and unselfish impulse. In the other cases it is more probable that expediency, or a conscious intention of paying for sins by *savabs*, entered into the matter.

To trace this peculiarity of the Yezdi's character to its source is not easy. Sometimes it appears to be a species of hedging, for it is very difficult to find out the truth in Persia, and a general disbelief in everything may have led the Persian to feel that it is unsafe to stake his all on one theory of the universe. The amount of lying that is done in a town like Yezd baffles description. An Englishman when in doubt tells the truth. A Persian when in doubt tells a lie. This would be more tolerable were it not that a Persian is always in doubt. In Yezd security is a thing unknown, and telling lies becomes part of the instinct of self-preservation. Then again the lies are of a new kind. Lies in England are generally told to deceive people in some particular; in Yezd they are just as frequently told in order to make the very search for truth impossible. When I have had to examine into cases of petty theft amongst schoolboys, I have found that to get at the truth is an almost superhuman task. English boys, if they do not tell the truth, will at least tell as few falsehoods as possible, if for no other reason, to avoid being found out. Persian boys will not only lie on the subject they wish to conceal, but they will tell as many untruths as they can cram into the story, so as to render any attempt at investigation futile. Of course you know that they are lying, but, as they never imagine that you will suspect them of telling the truth, they are not much deterred.

The result of this practice is that in the Yezd bazaars, taking together all statements, even the most trivial, that are made by Mussulmans, probably not less than one-third of the speeches made are falsehoods. I do not think that the Persian beggar ever expects to be believed. A woman once came to the house, asking for a quilt because she had none, and her son was ill. To have no quilt, that is, to have no bed-clothes, is by no means an unbelievable state of poverty, and there is no doubt that the woman expected to have her words taken literally. It transpired that her son was quite well, but was taking sanctuary to avoid being molested for a debt. The woman had a perfectly possible quilt, but it was old and patched. She actually brought it to us the next morning, not to prove that after all they were very poor, but to show that in saying she had none she had spoken the truth. Another woman once told me in the street, that she had six orphan children and her husband was sick.

In a country like this it is not surprising that evidence is at a discount, and that there are intelligent people absolutely convinced that truth is unknowable. A man who is accustomed to act upon this theory in the ordinary affairs of life, is naturally inclined to apply the same principle to whatever religion or philosophy he possesses. So we get men who are unwilling to stake everything on anything in particular. If they have previously assumed that it is most advantageous to do what is right, then it is well to perform just a few actions on the assumption that it is more advantageous to do wrong. If they have hitherto acted on the principle that it is better to do what is wrong, then it is well not to put all their eggs into that basket either. And indeed I am inclined to think that many of the Yezdis would apply the same philosophy to their non-ethical ideas. If they have based most of their opinions on the assumption that something is true, it is well to base others on the assumption that the same thing is false. This, of course, sounds to us mere nonsense, but once grant with many of the Yezdis that evidence is valueless, and truth absolutely unknowable, and it at once becomes an approximation to sense.

It is quite possible that some of my readers may ask whether this last attempt to explain the inconsistency of the Yezdis is to be taken seriously. To say that I do not know is rather a weak confession, but at the same time it is true. I certainly do not pin my faith to it, yet it seems to be the way in which the bewildering topsy-turvydom of Persia is working. Never forget that the jokes of W. S. Gilbert are the facts of Persia. For instance, in an isolated place like Yezd, the laws of supply and demand operate so peculiarly that the ordinary custom of discount on quantity is inverted; you will be able to get things usually sold at three for a penny at perhaps thirty for a shilling. There was a governor in Yezd, certainly not more than twenty years ago, who had men bastinadoed for walking in the bazaars without treading down the heels of their slippers. In such a country it is very difficult to say what is in itself ridiculous and impossible. One can only judge from evidence, which is, I think, in favour of the theory I have just suggested as a possible explanation of undoubted facts. At the same time the unreliability of the Yezdi is probably due to several causes, and there is one of these causes about which one may speak with less uncertainty. This is the piecemeal appreciation of ideas and circumstances, which I have already mentioned as the result of the impression made on the Yezdi's mind by the isolated objects which continually surround him, and which is probably heightened by a religion which was constructed under circumstances very similar to those of the Persian deserts.

Shame is the feeling of vexation consequent upon the consciousness of having fallen below an accepted standard of conduct, and where such a standard is not to be found, shame does not exist. Consequently the Yezdi, who has only the faintest idea of a moral standard that ought to govern his whole life, is not susceptible to shame in this particular. He has, however, a rather stronger idea of a general standard of intelligence up to which he ought to live, so it is often a greater deterrent to him to point out that a certain action will be regarded as ignorant or silly than to show that it is less moral than his ordinary behaviour. He also possesses a very keen appreciation of what he considers to be the ethical proprieties of a particular occasion. We must remember that what he lacks in breadth of view he makes up for in power of concentration on the comparatively small field of ideas that can come simultaneously within the range of his mental vision. For example, when European missionaries have been in vain attempting to simplify a most abstruse and metaphysical doctrine by spreading it over several easy steps, they sometimes find that the Persian mind, though it utterly fails to grasp the simpler train of reasoning, can without any assistance take in the more difficult idea, so long as it is expressed with sufficient brevity. In the same way the Yezdi, who seems to have little or no sense of the proprieties of a lifetime, will have an appreciation of what is right and fitting on a particular occasion stronger than that of the European. This is what makes him so dignified at times and seasons, and so undignified in his life. Although his sense of propriety does not always work, where it does work it is so far from being weak that to violate it seems to give him a sensation that is near akin to physical pain. You cannot make a Yezdi apologise: if he has done an injury, he is quite content to ignore it, or to assert that it has not taken place, which is the ordinary substitute for an apology in Persia: but the man's sense of shame is too great to allow him to confess to such an action before the man he has wronged. He has no objection to the man knowing what has happened; but at the interview his denial must be accepted or the injury ignored. This is the only way in which he can submit to the meeting.

The Yezdi has not a very fine sense of humour, but he is easily amused. Perhaps it is worth while to instance an occasion which occurred during our stay in Yezd when the natives seemed really tickled. A certain Russian doctor resident in the town, who had not a very complete and accurate knowledge of Persian, wanted to use bad language to his servant, who had in some way offended him. As he knew no suitable expressions he seized the dictionary and kept looking them out one after another, and hurled them at the unfortunate man's head as fast as this process would permit. This story was retailed with very great appreciation by some of the better class natives. I rather think it seemed to them very much more funny than it does to us, and this for two reasons. Persians have a great respect for literature, including dictionaries, and they would hardly understand their being frivolously handled; also they are very particular in adapting their language to the occasion, and it would strike them as the height of absurdity to abuse a servant in book language, as the doctor must have done, unless indeed the Russian publication he consulted contained real specimens of colloquial abuse, which would have struck the Persians as even more funny.

The story of Mulla Nāsiru'd Dīn and his mule is a very fair instance of Persian humour at its best. The Mulla, who was a notorious wit, had sent a mule to the market-place where such beasts were sold. People were suspicious owing to the Mulla's reputation, but nobody supposed that he would let himself down by sending an unsaleable animal to the bazaars. So first of all someone examined its forelegs, and got badly pawed; then someone went to its hind-legs and got kicked; next they looked at its mouth and got bitten; finally they tried to put saddle-bags on to its back, and it threw them off immediately. Consequently when the Mulla strolled down everyone laughed at him, and asked him if he really expected anybody to buy it. "No, my friends," said the Mulla, "I never expected any of you to buy it; but I wanted you to know what I have to put up with at home."

One of the things that is most difficult for a European to tolerate in a Yezdi is his extraordinary disregard of time. It is not only that he does not care how long he takes over a thing, one might tell story after story on this point, but this is a malady common in the East. What I was not prepared for was that he should have no idea what time means. In Persia a clergyman's work consists more of seeing people in his own house, and less of visiting; but the great difficulty in receiving visitors is that, if one wants to see parties separately, a single reception is all one can satisfactorily arrange in an afternoon. This is what happens. Two parties send to ask when they can see you, and you reply by asking when it will be convenient for them to come. Both messengers state with the most absolute politeness that it makes no difference to their masters when you say, and that they wish you to choose the time. If you are wise you will tell one party to come two hours after noon, and the other to come at one hour to sunset, which, supposing the sun to be setting at six, will be five o'clock. They will both acquiesce, but you will have to be ready to receive the party due at two at one o'clock, and you must not consider them late if they arrive at three. Similarly you will prepare for the second party at four, and not consider them late before six. But the probabilities are that both parties will arrive at four, the favourite visiting hour, having both decided on that time before sending to ask you. [5]

Another great difficulty is the Persian language. Persian is a pretty language with an extremely large vocabulary. What is more, every class of Yezdi, that is, of the men, uses a very large number of words. For all this it is almost impossible to accurately define an idea, for the language largely consists of synonyms, which cannot be used indiscriminately, but must be carefully selected according to the occasion. Some of these synonyms really possess accurate meanings, but if you choose your word according to the sense you wish to convey, you talk bad Persian. To give an illustration of this, suppose in dealing with the Incarnation you desired to bring out the Christian doctrine that God is not only the Friend of man but also his close Companion. I am quite certain that in ordinary Yezdi Persian there is no sufficiently appropriate term for "companion," that could be applied to God in such a way as to bring out your meaning, without exposing you to a charge of irreverence. As a matter of fact I once tried to convey this idea in a Persian sermon, and was met with this difficulty. I afterwards tried to get three or four native Christians, one of whom was a teacher of Persian, to suggest a possible word, but the only expression they could propose was the word I had used.

The words one uses in a letter in Persian, even for the commonest objects, are almost entirely distinct from the words one uses conversationally, and the words which one would use in an ordinary prose history book are again different. Then it is almost impossible to distinguish the tenses; the true future is hardly ever used, consequently the present and the future are indistinguishable; and the preterite is frequently used of action which was begun in the past but which is still continuing. Lastly, the adjective is generally indistinguishable from the substantive, and the link between an adjective and the term which it qualifies is the same as the sign of the genitive. For instance the text, "This is My beloved Son," may be read in the Persian Bible, "This is the son of My beloved" without the slightest violence to the grammar; nor, indeed, is there any obvious way out of the difficulty. I have mentioned these peculiarities of language because I think they are greatly connected with the Yezdi's inaccuracy of ideas, though which is the cause and which is the effect is sometimes difficult to say.

There is no situation in which the Yezdi is so incalculable as that which seems to demand a certain amount of daring. Sometimes the people seem absolutely wanting in the power of taking the initiative, and expect to be directed like children. They have an aversion to killing animals except for food, even when there is danger to human life in allowing them to live. One day an English lady asked why a dangerous dog which had bitten several people was not killed. The answer was, "If you tell us to kill it we will do so, but not otherwise." The fact is no one minded killing the dog, but they fancied the curse might lie with the initiator of the movement. They will go on letting things be, or allowing them to get more and more dangerous, until they have accustomed themselves to an amount of risk to incur which would be accounted by a European mere foolhardiness. In this they are largely influenced by predestinarian notions. An English lady was one day standing by an open tank in a Persian compound, into which one of the children had fallen that morning, and she remarked on its extreme danger. "Yes," said the mother, "I have lost three children in that tank." To build a small wall round such a tank would be in Persia exceedingly easy. Perhaps the little power of initiative that is left them by their predestinarianism is destroyed by the insecurity of the country. People get in the way of making as few improvements as possible, and of never exposing their capital more than they can help. In fraudulent business, however, there is a great deal of audacity, sometimes combined with a good deal of ingenuity. They are exporting at present to China a quality of so-called opium in which there is absolutely no morphia. The stuff is really an entirely different substance, and very cheap, and it is tied up in bags steeped in a solution of opium. It is, I believe, more harmful to smoke than the real article.

Passive courage the Yezdi possesses to a very high degree, but he must have a cause for which he cares sufficiently, if this courage is to be called out. If the terrible Babi massacres that have taken place from time to time in Persia have proved nothing else, they have at least shown that there is grit somewhere in Persian character. The way in which mere lads in Yezd went to their death in that ghastly summer of 1903 was wonderful. There was one boy whom they tried very hard to spare, for sometimes the mob were moved by something akin to pity. They took him to the *mujtahid* first, and told him to recant, and he would not. Then they took him to the open square, and held him up to give him one more chance, if he would curse the Behāu'llah and the Behāīs. "The curse be on yourselves," was all he said; and then they tore him in pieces. The early Babis showed good fighting qualities in the north of Persia, as well as passive courage, and, as they were chiefly townsmen, we may presume that there are military possibilities in the Persian people, even amongst those who dwell in cities. But to look for military feeling in the kind of soldier that we get in Yezd is not fair. He is, I believe, collected by a sort of conscription from certain localities. When collected he is taught about as much of the ordinary elements of drill as is considered necessary in England for the national schoolboy. He is also assigned a wage of a *toman* a month, which if punctually paid would be insufficient to cover anything but the barest food expenses. This mistake is, however, generally remedied by his superior officers, who usually intercept so much of his wages that he is bound to look for other means of support. In this he is not discouraged. If he has a little ready cash he usually sets up as a money-lender, his official position and possession of a bayonet assisting him to collect his debts. Otherwise he steals shoes, or takes up some other similar form of employment which does not demand an extensive capital; sometimes he even makes shoes. Once a year he is supposed to be supplied with a uniform, but, though the uniforms are probably not worth more than a few shillings, they are very seldom regularly supplied. He is, however, free to add to his uniform as well as to his pay, and at certain times of the year there is very little left of the original outfit except an old cap with a metal badge, and possibly a belt. When on sentry duty he amuses himself by planting a small garden, four inches by two, in front of his station, and he keeps a heap of rose-heads to press into the hands of passers-by on the chance of extracting odd halfpence.

During the latter days of the Babi massacres, a guard of four men, a sergeant and three privates, was placed at the doors of the European houses by the Governor. Every soldier came to us with a thing that looked like a gun and certainly had a bayonet attached to it; but we heard that at one house it became necessary to send down an extra weapon which would shoot for the common use of the party. Of course the gun that would shoot was withdrawn at the earliest possible opportunity. The higher officers of this extraordinary force are surprisingly numerous, but as there are among them, I believe, boys of about twelve who hold the title of Field-Marshal, there is some excuse for a reduplication of officers. It is only justice to add that some of these soldiers are in their way very good fellows: the guard sent to our house were by no means a bad lot; and I shortly afterwards met a military officer whom I would class with the best Persians I know.

Nor does the courage of Persia come out very strongly in the high official class, though here too there are honourable exceptions. Still, as a general rule, amongst those who claim nobility there is very little apprehension of the maxim "*noblesse oblige.*"

Of course there is in Yezdi manners and customs much that strikes the outsider as intensely funny. For instance, the etiquette is distinctly peculiar, and although very ceremonious, it does not always appear to the European to be characterised by great politeness. When you come into the room the first two minutes will be spent in phrases intended to convey an exaggerated respectfulness. In upper middle-class houses your host will take upon himself the menial offices of service, not only making your tea himself, but going out of the room every two minutes to supplement the crockery, or to fetch another lump of sugar. If you have a servant with you, your host or his other visitors will discourse freely with this man before your face as to your most trivial personal affairs, and if there is a pause in the conversation they will make side remarks to one another on the number of your virtues, and when they have discovered a certain consensus of opinion, they will turn to you and give you the benefit of it directly, by telling you that you are a very good man. From this you must not infer that Persian friendliness is hollow: all that can be said is that the etiquette is artificial. Even so it means something; for when a man is anxious to pay you proper respect he adheres to it closely, unless he has reason to suppose that you would like him to adopt something of European manners, which some Persians dealing with Europeans try to do. However the etiquette is too elaborate and artificial for universal use, and generally speaking it is not much used except in matters relating to visits and to letter-writing. On other occasions

Persians who have no intention of impoliteness are often a little off-hand as compared with other Easterns, and those who intend to be rude find plenty of opportunities for being so.

There is, I suppose, between the Persian and the European a difference of opinion as to what constitutes puerility. One of the Governors of Yezd once boasted to an English resident that it was no good trying to hide things from him, as he knew what every European in the town had for dinner. Then there is the custom of making absolutely worthless presents with the most superb *empressement*. Once when I was in a big village near Yezd with my wife and baby and mirza, a woman whom my wife knew came in, and after greeting us presented us with four very crumpled lettuce leaves, selecting the leaves according to her ideas of our exact precedence with the utmost care and circumspection, and having in the whole transaction very much the air of a maiden aunt giving a tip to a schoolboy. Nor must it be supposed that these customs only obtain amongst the women. A European banker once told me that if one of his brokers gave him anything, the others always followed his example; and that once at the bank one of them presented him with a rose-head, the second at once plunged his hand into his pocket and produced an old sweet, the third fumbled among his treasures, and at last found something which looked like a lump of gum. He could not quite remember what the fourth presentation was, but he fancied it was another sweet. Sometimes, particularly in Parsi houses, presents of this sort will be elaborately handed about, somewhat after the fashion of a round game, everybody giving something to everybody, and finishing with exactly the same amount as they had at the beginning. This game, however, is generally played on a special occasion, and the presents of fruit and sprigs of myrtle have a certain symbolical significance which gives grace and dignity to the performance. Of course the interchange of presents which although trifling have a positive value is one of the most striking features of the social intercourse of Persia. This is a custom which needs to be understood, and which soon degenerates into extravagance, but essentially it is a good custom. A higher value is always placed on what are called *saughāts* or travellers' presents, and Europeans either travelling or residing in Persia should remember that a certain number of these will be expected of them. When a Persian has done you a real civility, he feels that to a certain extent he has introduced you to his home, and any little European thing which you may give him he takes as a graceful introduction to your separate life, and he values it from this point of view much more than would be otherwise possible. The custom, however, has its drawbacks; for it is the fashion in Persia always to present anything which a visitor has admired, and this becomes a peculiarly hollow piece of etiquette. Occasionally big Persians in dealing with inferiors use this custom as a means of enriching themselves, but this of course is exceptional.

When all has been said I think that we must admit that for some reason or other the Persian is willing to expend his energies upon things which seem to us to be absolute trifles. This was curiously illustrated on one occasion by one of the Yezdi gentlemen who is supposed to have advanced most in civilisation and culture. I was calling at his house at the time, and he handed me a most elaborate atlas with charts and diagrams illustrating all sorts of out-of-the-way things. Some of these I did not feel myself competent to explain, but everything that I could explain he understood at once, and he had obviously before my arrival discovered the meaning of many of the diagrams. We passed on from this to discuss several of the great inventions of the age, including wireless telegraphy. In everything he showed a most intelligent interest, and great quickness of perception. Finally, he produced a photograph of a man who had been shown at an exhibition, I think at Paris. The man had an enormous beard, some twelve feet long. My Persian friend made no difference at all in his manner, but discussed this peculiar phenomenon in exactly the same way. I cannot remember all the details of this interview, or the exact amount of smile which my host allowed himself when we were discussing the photograph, but I have attempted to faithfully convey the general impression left on me by his manner. I think I am right in saying that it all points to the fact that the great difference between Persia and Europe is that the Persian tends to take things piecemeal, and the European to regard ideas in their relation to others. At the same time this is not always at once obvious. A European is firmly convinced of the value of scientific knowledge, and will decorate a man who has discovered all that is to be discovered about a black beetle. Here the Persian will laugh at the European, as he also will when the European rewards highly extreme excellence in the practical trivialities of life. But it is obvious that these exceptions are more apparent than real. The Persian is like a man who has got a pair of glasses that give him a very clear view of a very small field of vision. He does not view things absolutely piecemeal, but he generally regards only a very small area at a time. A man who picks up shells with an idea of adding to the general store of human knowledge is to him an imbecile; but he is only willing to pay the same attention to an invention like Marconi's that he would to an improved hair-wash. The consequence is that the Yezdi very soon adapts himself superficially to circumstances, and it is very easy to veneer him, but he does not easily assimilate fresh principles of action. In dealing with Persians it is well to realise this, and not to build too much on their adaptability.

A Persian visitor, when he is behaving according to strict etiquette, depreciates not only himself but all his belongings. It has been suggested that the admiration which is frequently expressed for foreign customs and ideas is really due to this etiquette, and similarly that the belittling of Persia as a country that has gone to pieces is due to the same cause. This suggestion is, I believe, entirely incorrect. A Yezdi will belittle himself, his house, his relations, and the country of Persia, because he regards the first three as purely personal, and does not care the least bit about the fourth; but if he belittles his town, his etiquette, or the foundations of his creed, he will make it very plain that he expects you to understand that he simply does it out of civility. There is one thing that a Yezdi puts before everything, and that is the water-supply of his town. I personally got on very well with the Yezdis, although I had to own that I did not admire Mohammed or his religion. But another European, who openly stated that he did not approve of their water, succeeded in absolutely alienating their affections. These exceptions show that Yezdis are willing to exhibit their pride in what they really love. They are also very proud of their literature, their language, and their intelligence. As a matter of fact, considering their extreme ignorance, they are not a conceited people, and their willingness to adopt foreign things more or less points to the same conclusion. Some of them, and these are generally the most ignorant, are insufferably conceited, but as a rule their comparative freedom from this vice makes them peculiarly likeable.

The nearest approach to a moral principle that I can find amongst the Persians is their commendation of simple acts of kindness. As I have before mentioned the idea of *savabs* covers many actions which have no ethical point, and it fails to cover in the Persian mind many actions of a moral character where the benefit is not at once apparent. But Yezdis are brought up to admire simple and direct acts of kindness, and to enjoy doing them. Generally speaking, they are very good-natured, and in nothing is this so obvious as in their conduct towards children. Of course cases of gross cruelty to children come to one's notice occasionally, but they are after all the exception and not the rule, and the children are more often spoilt by weak indulgence. The Yezdi's conduct towards animals very well illustrates his character. I believe that there is less wanton cruelty, particularly towards wild animals, than you would find in a European town. On the other hand, the cruelty towards working beasts is beyond description, there being in this case an ulterior object. Again, the dogs in the street, which are more or less under the ban of the Mussulman religion, are treated in the most extraordinary way. They are made the recipients of little acts of good-natured kindness, perhaps under the impression that a *savab*, even to a dog, cannot do any harm, perhaps because a Yezdi is often better than his ideas. They are also treated on occasions with the most fearful cruelty, and the cruelty in this case has no point but the satisfaction of a religious prejudice. This is, after all, exactly the way in which the Yezdi Mussulman treats the human being whom he considers unclean. He has alternative principles which he chooses according to his mood and circumstances. Sometimes the prejudice against killing animals gives rise to very great cruelty. It is generally considered a sin to kill an animal except in self defence or for food, but you may do anything to it short of extinguishing life with your own hand.

To sum up, in the case of offences against the person Yezdis have an inkling of an ethical principle, which is frequently at issue with the more explicit teaching of their religion. This seems to me to be one of the most hopeful points in Persian character, and one which the missionary ought to most carefully study, trying to make it in many cases the basis of his appeals. But we have to beware of trading too much upon this very rudimentary principle. When we come to offences against property, we shall find it applied much less frequently, and working with much less force. There is no inclination to honesty in a Mussulman's character to correspond with the inclination to kindly action. If you want to find anything of this kind you must go to the Parsis. On the contrary, there is nothing that gives the Yezdi Mussulman such intense satisfaction as the feeling that he has scored by his wits. He would much rather steal one *kran* than earn two by the same expenditure of effort. A certain amount of dishonesty is recognised, and is not in any way resented. The servants, for instance, expect to make a certain profit upon all transactions. The extent of their profit is by custom left entirely to the conscience of the servant, but everybody would confess that taking more than a certain amount was wrong. You will frequently catch less trustworthy servants trying to make over fifty per cent., and sometimes over a hundred. As to the morality of this custom when the lowest possible percentage is drawn I can only say that I am not wholly convinced, as it appears to me that servants who are trying to live a straight life never ask for it to be sanctioned, and sometimes certainly give it up, at any rate in its direct form. But the point is that wages are generally arranged on a scale that allows for a man taking very much more than the minimum percentage. Nor is this sort of allowance for dishonesty only made in servants' wages. One day the cook of one of the Europeans went to the bazaars for meat, and after the usual haggling the price was fixed at twelve *krans* a *man'* (thirteen pounds), "But," said the cook, "you have got your thumb on the scale." "And do you think," retorted the butcher, "that I am going to give you meat at twelve *krans* a *man'*, unless I keep my thumb on the scale?" This shows you something of Persian business principles, and indeed trickery is regarded by all Persians as part of the ordinary routine of life. Our servant once asked the milkman if he could sell us some cream, and the man replied quite gravely, "No, if I take off the cream they will complain of the milk."

He obviously thought that the natural way to supply us with cream would be to skim the milk he sold us.

Passing to the merchant class the opium trade affords a good instance of the most barefaced type of wholesale fraud. Indeed, the fraud of a Persian town is beyond conception. We had a neighbour in Yezd who was considered a fairly respectable man, and whose sole business was the forging of seals. But the fact is that every class, from the highest to the lowest, is thoroughly permeated by the leaven of dishonesty.

There is so little security for property in Persia that men do not consider it worth their while to amass wealth by ordinary means. Everybody in a town like Yezd is trying to effect a *coup*, either a big one or a small one, and one of the results is the most extraordinarily rapid shifting of social positions. In Persia the road from beggary to princedom is a very short one, and the road from princedom to beggary is not very lengthy; only in this return journey it is somewhat difficult to prevent being assassinated, for when a big man is disgraced his life is in extreme danger.

This inattention to ordinary and petty business enterprise has curious results. When I first went to Yezd I found it almost an impossibility to get the things I wanted from the bazaars. The European has to deal with the bazaar through his servants, and it took my men about three days to get the commonest articles other than necessary provisions. Articles which I knew would need a little hunting for were sometimes, if I insisted, procured within the month. This is absolutely without exaggeration; and, although I believe I was unfortunate, other residents and travellers in Persia have confessed to similar difficulties. You may go into a town where the chief occupation is weaving, and declare that you want some of the woven articles which it is their principal business to make, and it is very possible that you may be unable to procure them, or only able to get the most inferior specimens, if you are passing through quickly. This is rather less true of the larger places on the main roads, like Tehran and Isfahan, but in towns like Yezd there is the greatest difficulty in getting what you want.

In an emergency it is frequently almost impossible for a European to get what is needed, if the things required are not such as he has been accustomed to buy at other times. To offer rather more than the price one usually gives is not of much use, and frequently has the very reverse effect to what is intended; for the seller in such a case may decide to forego the profits of legitimate trading for the chances of effecting a *coup*. But the real difficulty is rather that the retail trading of Yezd is totally devoid of ordinary enterprise. When the trader moves out of the ordinary rut of his every-day commerce he prefers to be fraudulent. In his customary business the shop-keeper makes a fair profit, and although his dealings may not be very extensive, there is always the chance of something really good coming his way. Meanwhile he has a position very much more dignified than that of the English shop-keeper. In Yezd the seller, not the buyer, is the conferrer of the benefit, and so far as the relation is concerned, the superior. When he sells very small quantities, he often charges less than the usual price. When he sells large quantities, he frequently charges something extra. Europeans in an ordinary way have not much difficulty in getting regular supplies when they become well known, though they have to pay more for them than the natives do. An Armenian also has to pay more than a Yezdi, but less than a European. I am inclined to think that the poorer natives suffer from the difficulty of procuring on emergencies things which they do not ordinarily buy quite as much as ourselves, though probably the richer Persians have more facilities. This is just one specimen of the inertia of Yezd. In matters of transport one is even more in the hands of other people. It is extremely difficult to find transport at less than three days' notice, and one can seldom get off on a journey within two hours of the time arranged. During the journey there is the same difficulty in controlling affairs. Under such circumstances people naturally get a tendency towards fatalism, and undue persistence even gets to be regarded as a sin. Probably this has some effect on the religious conceptions of the people, for, if a man who sticks to his point is not to be admired, it is difficult to understand why we should consider unchangeableness of purpose a necessary attribute of the Deity. Whatever may be the orthodox doctrine of Islam upon the subject, there is no doubt that the Yezdi fails utterly to understand why there should be any persistence or consistency in the view taken by the Deity of human sin, for the Yezdi himself would hardly feel justified as a father, or person in authority, in taking a similar firm stand. One of the consequences of this doctrine is that weakness is hardly accounted a sin at all. I remember two conversations with Babi mullas in which this came out very forcibly. They tried to argue that *taqīyu*, that is, the custom of denying one's faith under the stress of danger, was sanctioned in the gospels by the story of Peter's denial. I have also found other Persians who have disputed the sinfulness of Peter's action, on the ground that he was the victim of compulsion. But the most curious suggestion with regard to the defensibility of weak conduct was made by another party of Babi mullas, who considered that the difference between the forbearance of Christ towards His enemies and the impatience exhibited by Mohammed was fully accounted for by the respective lengths of their ministries.

One finds the marks of this want of persistence everywhere. I have seldom seen a tombstone in Yezd that has been finished accurately, and there is scarcely a building that has not got a rough, unfinished corner. Similarly every one who has seen a Persian carpet knows that the design is almost always broken in at least one place.

I suppose the *prima facie* conclusion is that the Yezdi is the weakest of weak beings, but I am very doubtful whether this conclusion is true. Repose and weakness are two different things, and although we seldom find the Yezdi putting out his strength, the condition of the country is hardly such as to rouse him. Certainly in the sphere of morals the Yezdi's religion gives him very little inducement to a consistent life. "The Light That lighteth every man that cometh into the world" is not wanting in Persia. Sometimes it makes Mussulmans superior to their creed, but, if I may be allowed to express an opinion, I think this Light operates more in calling men out of Islam than in guiding them in it.[6] I should hesitate to make a similar statement about the Parsis. It is not my intention to discuss Zoroastrianism at length, but although it is a religion without a gospel, almost all the essential ideas about God, and right and wrong, and the bases of human action are undoubtedly true so far as they go.

If one wants to know whether the Yezdi Mussulman is strong or weak, one must examine his conduct when he is sure of his cause. I think he is worthy of some praise for the self-restraint he habitually shows when he is conforming to the by no means easy restrictions of an established and elaborate etiquette. But, as I have previously said, the thing which has opened people's eyes to the enormous strength of Persian character under partially favourable moral conditions, is the way in which the Babis have exposed themselves to martyrdom, and have stood firm to their beliefs and cause under tortures too horrible for description. It has been mentioned that, although Yezdis, while they remain Mussulmans, do not show any great enthusiasm for a distinction between right and wrong, they still possess the greatest powers of loyalty both to causes and to individuals. In their affection for those for whom they care they are anything but weak, and when they really attach themselves to Christianity and realise the personal presence of Christ, they develop an unexpected strength of character. We must, however, beware of expecting an utter change of constitution to take place at the time of conversion.

A Yezdi's personal attachments do not run so closely along the lines of duty and relationship as might be expected by people coming to Persia from other Eastern countries. The family tie is not always a very strong one, though it is sometimes exceedingly strong. Perhaps one reason for this is the extreme looseness of matrimonial relations. A Shiah may have four regular and permanent wives. When he marries, a settlement is made on the woman, who may be divorced at any time if he cares to pay the settlement. The woman may also divorce her husband, if she cares to forfeit the settlement, that is if she is sufficiently mistress of her own movements to be able to make the necessary arrangements. There is no limit to the number of divorces and re-marriages, so long as no man possesses at any time more than four wives. Besides these he may have as many temporary wives as he likes. It is true that these wives are theoretically only slaves, but this, after all, is simply a legal quibble. They can be married either for a few days or for a few years. Babis may only have one wife, and divorce is discouraged, though amongst the less respectable Babis in Yezd divorce is as common as anywhere. Some of the more respectable Mussulmans in Yezd openly profess a belief that monogamy is the more respectable state, and among the better Yezdi merchants it is very common. Girls are sometimes married extremely young, for instance at nine or ten, but there is a growing feeling that to marry a very young child is not altogether respectable, and some of the better class merchants prefer not to let their girls be married before fourteen. Of course this is an unsatisfactory state of things, but one must not fly to the conclusion that there is no affection in Persian marriages. One of the missionaries had a lad of about eighteen in his employment, and there had been talk of a marriage between him and a child of ten or twelve. Going home one evening for his night off, he found that he had landed in the middle of his own marriage ceremony, which took place that night. He was a good-natured lad, fond of children, and the little wife was devoted to him and was terribly distressed at his not coming home the next night, for she had got everything ready for him, and would not believe he was not coming. When one of the ladies from the missionary's house went to call on her some days after she came very close up and whispered that she wanted her husband to come home every night.

The women of the highest official class are kept very close in Yezd, perhaps only going out once in six months, except to the bath; but the merchants' wives have considerably more liberty, and the commoner women go about freely. Sometimes there is a great deal of real affection in the home, at other times exceedingly little, especially when there is more than one wife, and sometimes there is the grossest cruelty. The fact is that Persians are led by impulse in these matters. They are very slightly constrained by any feeling of principle. As a class perhaps the old mothers are the worst treated, and an old woman generally prefers going to her daughter rather than to her son. One of the richest merchants in Yezd had an old mother who was very ill, and he refused even to buy a chicken to make the broth the doctor had ordered. At last a favourite black slave wheedled one out of him, and made the broth for the old woman. Slaves in Persia are very valuable and are generally well treated. On the other hand, another well-known merchant and landowner, whose old mother-in-law was very ill, thought nothing too good for her; he insisted on her having all she wanted promptly, and came himself to her room at least once a day to enquire after her health. The same man took a personal interest in seeing that every provision was made for the comfort of his old cook when she was past work, and the general tone of the household was one of affection and consideration. Another big merchant, whose old mother had fallen off a roof, showed the very greatest solicitude for her comfort in every possible way, spending hours with her, and himself lifting her most carefully. At the same time the old women as a class are not well treated, and in the better class houses it is often difficult to distinguish them from the servants. The poorer classes are generally no better. I remember that at one time my wife was trying to explain to one of my servants' wives what ingratitude meant. The woman was very fond of her children, so my wife asked, "Would you not think it very ungrateful, if, when you were old and poor, your boy refused to do anything for you?" "No," she said, "of course that is what I expect. Our boys are always like that. We only say, 'It is the will of God.'" Several women present joined in the laugh at my wife's ignorance.

Of course a great deal of cruelty goes on in the less respectable Persian households, and the use of poison is not uncommon. It should be explained that in Persia people who are not even professedly respectable are to be found in every class, and in a commercial town like Yezd status goes largely by wealth, and carries with it no obligation to keep up even a superficial reputation. The organisation of the household is very largely outside the operation of the ordinary law. I do not know what is the exact legal limit of the *jus paternum*, but I am quite sure that it is very difficult to bring to book the head of a household for murdering any member of his family. Also in the case of a member of the family leaving Islam, the matter would probably be primarily left to the head of the household, although if the case was flagrant the matter might also be taken up by outsiders. It is very necessary to understand this when discussing the possibility of religious liberty in Persia. Religious liberty, proclaimed by a firman of the Shah, would not have the enormous value which is sometimes supposed. Indeed it would be almost entirely without immediate value, unless the Persian government were considerably strengthened, and a limitation put on the *jus paternum*. A decision by leading *mujtahids* that it was expedient to give such liberty either to the individual or to the family, would probably have more immediate effect, but, even were such a thing possible, it would be difficult to say how long such a decision would remain unchanged if advantage was really taken of it, and the precedent of the decision would on the whole be rather a bad one.

Another conceivable form of religious liberty is that the right of making converts from Islam should be secured by treaty to the European missionary. This, however, would not put a stop to the persecution of converts. There is so much injustice that is done in Persia as a matter of course, that it would be very difficult to prove that Persian subjects who were converts had been interfered with for religious reasons. One of the difficulties that missionaries experience at present, is that converts are always bringing forward instances of injustice which they themselves believe to be due to their profession of Christianity, whereas the missionary, who has considerable doubts on the subject, is often afraid of calling down real persecution by using his influence on their behalf.

The subject of religious liberty is a very difficult one, and although some people feel that an extension of treaty rights would be a good thing, and others, that a firman of the Shah giving religious liberty to his subjects would help the growth of sound and civilised ideas in his domain, there can be no doubt that the primary want is strong and good government. I have tried in this chapter not to discuss the government of Persia more than is absolutely necessary. It is of course far from perfect. At the same time, during my stay in Yezd, the governors of the town, and notably the Jalālu'd Daula, showed great friendliness to the whole European colony, and great fairness in their attitude towards the mission. The strengthening of the Persian government is a clear gain to the missionary, and seeing that strong government without religious liberty could certainly do for us infinitely more than religious liberty without strong government, I personally feel that the strengthening of the Persian government, central and local, is at present the main desideratum. At the same time, with God all things are possible, and I should hesitate to press this view on other people.

One or two instances of the lengths to which crime can go in Persian houses without arousing much notice from the authorities might be recorded. There was in Yezd one man who stabbed his own child in its mother's arms, and remained absolutely unpunished. He was still flagrantly ill-treating his wife and children while we were in the town. In the Isfahan district, a man murdered his child-wife by pouring paraffin over her and lighting it. The child died in the Julfa hospital. If any punishment was inflicted it was a very light one. There was another woman in Yezd dangerously stabbed by her son-in-law, but as she did not die, even her family took very little notice of the matter. These are a few typical specimens of the way in which the family is allowed to manage, or mismanage, its own affairs.

SQUARE OUTSIDE GOVERNOR'S RESIDENCE IN YEZD.

Generally speaking, Yezdis are open-handed. They have not the least shame about begging, and will show the greatest meanness in money-getting, but this does not prevent their being themselves generous at times. The fact is, that they regard beggary as a bargain; one man gets a coin, and the other a *savab*. They accept kindnesses of any sort in this manner, and consider that they give as good as they get, particularly if they are Seyids; but for all this, they are frequently ready to take the other side in the game. Probably not less than ten per cent of the population are professional beggars, and as they do not starve, we may conclude that a great deal of money is given away. But the open-handedness of the Yezdi takes other forms besides the mere giving of money to those who ask for it. He spends money freely upon his own pleasures: considering his poverty he lives well: this is true of all classes: finally, he really enjoys showing hospitality.

There is in Persian hospitality a great deal more than the observance of etiquette. Even the inquisitiveness of the Yezdi is a kind of attempt to get into real touch with his guest. In a word, he is essentially human. Most Europeans who have lived in Persia find it rather difficult to explain why they like the people. In the Yezdi there is certainly much to lament, but there is something to admire, and very much more to like. A people who are open-handed, good-natured, affectionate, not always extravagantly conceited, and above all, intensely human, are a people one cannot help getting to like when one lives among them for any time. At the same time, their inquisitiveness, unpunctuality, intense dishonesty, frequent ingratitude, and absolute want of principle in everything, are, to say the least of it, very trying. As to their exact position in the scale of civilisation, my personal opinion of them greatly changed after living through the Babi massacre of 1903. To find men, and women too, who had been to a certain extent influenced by contact with Western ideas and standards, and who prided themselves on representing the section of Persian Society most advanced in civilisation and refinement, openly gloating over horrors that would pollute these pages if I were to write them, seemed to us to be an indication of a more radical difficulty than was evidenced by the horrors themselves. At the same time, the behaviour of the Babis under persecution was sufficient to convince any one that there is plenty of strength in the Persian character, if only it can be called out.

My conclusion is that it is unfair to the Yezdi's character to in any way depreciate the evil effects of the circumstances among which he lives. His want of principle, his ferocity, and other similar points in his character can most of them be traced to a religious system which was forced upon him by the sword; for we must remember that he is four-fifths a Parsi, and only one-fifth an Arab. The good points in his character are much less easy to trace to his religion. He is not indisposed to reform, a fact which is proved by the success of the Babi movement, the possibilities of which have been discussed already.

Under these circumstances one can hardly imagine a country where the call to Christian missionary work was so peremptory, both because of the need and because of the peculiar opening afforded. Missionary work must, of course, be based rather upon the direct commandment of the Saviour than upon human judgment. However, there is no doubt that God sometimes accentuates His written commands by placing peculiar circumstances before our eyes, and I cannot conceive places appealing more strongly to the intelligent student of the missionary field than these isolated towns of Persia, one of which I have attempted to describe.

CHAPTER VI

From what has been previously said it will be understood that from the missionary point of view there are, when dealing with the Persian, certain peculiar difficulties, and also certain things which tend to make missionary work more easy. We have to deal with a people whose fundamental notions of God and of His dealings with men are absolutely different from our own. I am not now so much speaking of those tenets on which the Mussulman loves to dwell, but rather of those tenets of which he does not think it necessary to speak, which are not so much the objects of his faith, but rather indisputable facts which stand outside the sphere of faith. The difficulty is not so much that the Persian is repelled by our holding contrary ideas; he cannot believe that we hold them; and indeed it is a serious difficulty that in accepting the Persian language we often unconsciously admit the very Mussulman ideas which we intend to attack, and give to the Persian premises upon which he can build his whole argument. To give an illustration; a Persian enquirer will say to the missionary, "Of course you allow that Moses and David were prophets?" The missionary will probably admit this. Now if the Persian has used the most ordinary term for such prophets, that is, the term *paighambar*, he will naturally suppose that the missionary has admitted the following: first of all, that God sends from time to time men who are appointed by Him to reveal a new law of human action, which, so far as the moral commandments are concerned, has no necessary connection with previous revelation; secondly, that Moses and David gave each of them a sufficient direction to the peoples of their day to enable them to apprehend salvation. In all probability your Mussulman friend will assume that you have granted even more; for instance, that Moses and David were both of them commissioned to invite everyone they came across to accept their religion; and I should be sorry to say that you would not have been supposed to have made other still more impossible admissions.

I do not think that it would be possible to avoid this difficulty by extreme scrupulosity in accepting terms. The result of such hesitation would probably be to puzzle and perplex the sincere enquirer who was genuinely anxious to find out what Christianity really meant. A more possible way out of the difficulty is to take the first opportunity of stating the difference between Mussulman and Christian belief upon these subjects, and I shall perhaps be pardoned for suggesting that such matters ought to be thoroughly thought out beforehand. There are a good many terms that we use in the present day, such as "perpetuity of the moral law," and "continuity and growth of revelation," which require very careful analysis before they can be presented to minds which have not been accustomed to the ideas they represent. I have previously compared the mind of the Yezdi to a field-glass of very small range and high power, and have pointed out that the man possessing such a glass sees very clearly within a limited area. The Yezdi is utterly different from the European. The latter looks for a generally consistent system, and, knowing how difficult it is to get such a thing, he is content to find certain points where the agreement has not been thoroughly worked out. The typical Yezdi expects a much more clearly worked out conception of that small number of points which are at one time presented to his range of vision. But when he has turned his glasses in another direction the first set of ideas is blotted out, and the second group as a whole may be absolutely contradictory to the first, so long as it is consistent in itself. The result is that he is absolutely untouched by criticism which appears to the European crushing and final. Then the missionary gets to regard him as an imbecile, and presents to him an idea which he has not clearly thought out himself. The Persian turns the tables on him in a moment, and frequently the missionary is greatly surprised. The only way to meet this difficulty is both to prepare and select your arguments carefully, and, generally speaking, you can never use with the ordinary Shiah Mussulman an argument that contains more than three steps. As to the difficulties of the language, some have been previously mentioned, and to these must be added the entire absence of words conveying certain important conceptions. Perhaps we are not quite so badly off as the missionary to the Esquimaux, who has to explain our Lord's parables to people who know of hardly any domestic animals at all, and who have never seen a tree; nor is the Persian so intensely dull as the inhabitants of the Indian district where the mirzas declared that the meaning of the "field to bury strangers in" could not possibly be understood unless the strangers were described as dead; but to find a people who are sufficiently advanced to have an elaborate system of psychology, and yet have no term for conscience is a difficulty of almost a new kind. Between this sort of deficiency on the one hand, and on the other the impossibility of forming a sentence with an accurate meaning, or of making the meaning understood when it is formed, the missionary is sometimes inclined to wish the Persian language at the bottom of the sea.

A very similar difficulty is to be found in the absolute denial, especially by the Babis, of any limitations to the use of parabolic language. I can best explain this by instancing a very common Babi argument, by which it is attempted to minimise the extraordinary nature of Christ's ministry, this being a preparatory step to the advancement of the claims of Behāu'llah. Christ on one occasion said, "Let the dead bury their dead." In this text it is obvious that the word "dead" refers in one case rather to spiritual than to physical death. Consequently, they say, the miracles of raising the dead to life which are recounted in the Gospels are not to be taken as referring to physical death either. The obvious answer, that parabolic language, when used without any warning and under circumstances that make it certain to be interpreted as literal statement, is simply another name for falsehood, entirely fails to appeal to the Persian mind, even though it is pointed out in addition that, in the stories of the raising of the dead, local colour and special circumstances are added in such a way that the details of the stories do not admit of any intelligible allegoric interpretation.

In meeting this kind of position the difficulty is occasionally increased by the Babi controversialist being aware that certain European objectors hold a very similar opinion about our Lord's ministry. I think, however, that I am right in saying that no European critic has ever attempted to take up what seems to us the impossible position of accepting the absolute truth and inspiration of the New Testament, which the Babi fully admits, while at the same time trying to explain away the plain statements of the Gospels.

Another difficulty is that some, and those not always the least intelligent, of the Yezdi enquirers mistrust absolutely all reported evidence. This is after all only the logical result of life in a Persian town. To say that a certain point, even the most elementary, such as the fact of our Lord's appearance in Palestine nineteen hundred years ago, is a matter of history, or is universally acknowledged, means to the Yezdi absolutely nothing. Sometimes, however, when you are able to explain that historical criticism is not an impossibility in Europe, this extreme scepticism partially subsides, particularly when you are able to show that the demand for direct evidence is not altogether impossible to satisfy.

Of course, too, there are difficulties in argument arising from the intense ignorance of the Yezdi, and more particularly from his extremely limited ideas of the size of the world. For instance, when he is repeating the story that the text of the Bible was changed in the time of Mohammed, the verses referring to the prophet being eliminated, it is almost impossible to explain the enormous difficulty that would have attended such a proceeding. This must of course be the case in other places, but I venture to think that the peculiar nature of the Persian desert towns makes this state of mind compatible with a greater degree of intelligence than one would have believed possible.

When everything has been said, the strong attachment felt by the Yezdi to Islam remains the greatest difficulty of all. It has been previously shown that Islam is much more than a creed, and much more than a set of commandments. Behind these things are a number of more or less connected ideas upon the relations of God and man, which have not only been accepted without question for generations, but are considered by the Mussulman to be axiomatic and impossible to call in question. Also around Islam there has grown up a system of domestic and social life and of personal habit, which fills up every moment of the day. Habits of personal cleanliness, the system of cooking food, the fashion of dress, and the method of speech are all more or less connected with Islam. The same thing is true of the more normal amusements of the Yezdi. There is a certain amount of singing and playing which is in direct contravention of Mohammedan law; but the things which in the life of the people take the place of the concert-hall and of the theatre are the *ruza-khani*, which is the recitation of religious poems by the Mohammedan mulla, and the Muharram festival, which is entirely religious, being a miracle-play depicting the martyrdom of the Imam Husain. Even the more usual street shows, which are presented by story-telling dervishes, are the property of a class possessing a peculiar religious status. Under these circumstances who can wonder that to separate himself from Islam without leaving the country seems to the enquirer almost impossible? Further, he is inclined to say that, if it is possible, it is only to be done by joining himself to the life of the Ferangi household. It is very difficult to explain to the Mussulman that Christianity is not a politico-religious system like Islam, but it is still more difficult to make him understand that a certain amount of the Islamic system can in any way remain lawful to him when he becomes a Christian.

The difficulty is really an enormous one. Men who would be ready to face death, if death was in the air, are not always ready to face boycott and petty persecution, their neighbours regarding them as unclean, and their new co-religionists, though not refusing to associate with them, having apparently no idea of providing them with a new home atmosphere. Those, too, who are dependent on their professions or trades feel that as Christians the friction with Islam will be so great that, even if they are not treated as infidels and at once turned adrift, their seeking of their livelihood will be a daily martyrdom, often extremely distressing to their newly-awakened religious feelings.

All of the obvious solutions of this problem are almost as difficult as the difficulty itself. First of all, it might be possible to create an industrial mission, and to provide new employment and new circumstances of life for the converts. Such a move would attract so much attention in a town like

Yezd that it might very possibly provoke a serious riot; and, even if it did not do this, it would involve an enormous financial loss. It would be impossible to get for such an enterprise the sympathy of the Persian authorities. The undertaking would be attacked by a continual succession of intrigues, and even without these disadvantages it is doubtful whether Europeans who had to deal with Persians in matters of trade without being primarily traders could possibly avoid bankruptcy after a very short period. Besides this if any such plan was started, the possibilities of the situation from the employé's point of view would so appeal to the Persian that numbers would come and profess conversion in order to reap their share in the benefits. It cannot be too fully pointed out that in Yezd the man who is not in earnest, and who is willing to deny sincerity of motive, risks absolutely nothing, even though he may consent to public or semi-public ceremonies.

Another solution of the difficulty is to employ converts in the missionaries' households, but after all this only provides for a certain number, and those only of certain classes. If the less satisfactory servants and employés were continually ousted to make room for converts, a further very serious difficulty would be created, as there would be a number of people in the town doing their best to stir up trouble. The position is further complicated by the number of servants in a Persian household being very much fewer than the usual number in an Indian one. At the same time this solution of the difficulty, when it is possible, is certainly the best one. Converts who are employed by Christians are in South Persia a far from unsatisfactory class, particularly when they have given up more remunerative work. When the converts are left too much to fend for themselves the results are not always satisfactory, for even when they pull through, a feeling of not having been properly treated is sometimes left behind, which is not helpful to their Christian life. Consequently, I feel that, at the present stage, converts should, when possible, be drawn carefully into the organisation of the mission or the mission households, which would also have the effect of increasing the missionary staff. If it is due to our faith in Christ, as it most surely is, to send out every European man or woman who comes forward for mission work, and after prayerful and careful examination or training still seems to be set apart for that work by God, surely in the Persian mission under present circumstances we might receive as fellow-workers those who after accepting the Gospel are thrown upon our hands by the same God. Later on it may become possible to connect the Persian mission stations with an industrial organisation at Bombay, or God may show some other similar way out of the apparent *cul-de-sac*. But the whole difficulty is so great, that perhaps it would be well to keep it in mind when we are determining the organisation of missions, for some methods of work tend to absorb natives of various classes, while others show no tendency to do so. In spite of the immense difficulties in the way of regular industrial missions, some Persian missionaries hold that they ought to be started, under the charge of thoroughly competent men sent out for the purpose. My personal opinion is that, if it was the main intention that such work should lead to the formation of an industrial community of converts earning their own living and paying their own expenses, there would probably be a great deal of disappointment about the results. If, however, such work was attempted it would have to be done in very close conjunction with the strongest of the medical missions, and a responsibility for backing it up would have to rest with the doctors in charge. On the other hand, the establishment of industrial training classes under competent teachers, not necessarily European, would not be open to the same objections. It would really be a development of school work, and the primary object would be the assistance of the native population and the spreading of the Gospel message amongst them. Like other branches of mission work it would be worked at as small a loss as possible. But it would not be a settlement of the great difficulty, though we might reasonably expect it to prove a step towards such a settlement, for it would obviously put us in a position to consider further steps as occasion offered. After all, missionary work is the attempting of the impossible in dependence on the Almighty, and under such circumstances to attempt to look too far ahead is absurd.

In the face of these difficulties it is really wonderful that missionary work in Yezd should have gone so far forward. There are, of course, certain elements in Yezdi character and ideas that have proved a very great assistance to the missionary. Yezdis are always ready to talk about religion, and they are thoroughly sociable. Then they are always interested in new ideas, and are quick to adapt themselves to circumstances. Further, the ordinary Shiah's ideas about the Bible, that is, the Law of Moses and the Gospel, are somewhat uncertain. He generally regards it as the Word of God, for he does not consider that the alterations which he believes to have been made in the text are sufficient to rob the Book of its whole value. Altogether, his ideas are much less stereotyped than those of the Sunni, and it is often possible to convince him that the Book is correct throughout.

Then there is the extreme intelligence of the Shiah in grasping single points. Some missionaries work upon this, and also on his essential weakness, by teaching him Christian ideas, and not pointing out their contradiction to those contained in Islam until he has had time to grasp their value. I am inclined to think that although this method of teaching may be possible with people who do not come primarily as enquirers, it is not so suitable for the Yezdi who comes to you for discussion or teaching on the Christian religion. If you want to gain a particular point with a Persian, for instance if you wish to dissuade him from some particular act of cruelty, do not use too long an argument, but put what you want to say and your reasons for saying it as shortly as possible. Even if he does not recognise your principle generally, he may very possibly accept it for the particular occasion, if your argument is a plain and short one; but when an enquirer after Christianity comes to you, he comes to you as to a follower of Christ. He does not want your advice about any particular part of his conduct; he wants to know why you follow Christ rather than Mohammed. As a matter of fact you have to teach him more, but the attempt to teach him less generally produces a strange state of bewilderment, in which the man is not very likely to obey any explicit direction you may have given him. The man wants, not necessarily controversy, but teaching of a controversial nature, opposed to Mohammedanism, that is to the doctrine of the supremacy of Mohammed's religion, and he generally wants such teaching to be based on some kind of argument, and not on mere assertion. I think this last statement is less true of the women. But in our early days at Yezd, when Dr White and I were both struggling with the Persian language, and all of the teaching had to be done by Armenian hospital assistants, who, although admirable fellows, had perhaps not wholly grasped exactly what was wanted, we had strong evidence of what I am now saying. For the moment I could speak the language and began to see something of the people, man after man would come to me, all with the same question, "We have heard a great deal; a great deal of Christian teaching, and a great deal about Jesus Christ; but Sahib, *matlab chīst?*" which may be translated, "What is the point of it all?"

From what has been written it will be obvious that one of the most essential points in dealing with Persian visitors is to understand thoroughly who are enquirers and who are not. Those who are not primarily enquirers may often be brought to Christianity almost as easily as those who come as searchers after truth, for when you get to know Persians, you can do much with them through personal influence, and indeed, when all has been written about ways and methods, the thing most used of God in Persia is the personality of particular missionaries. Curiously enough, it is not always the popular personality by which the Persian is most affected in big matters, but he is enormously affected by what we call character. As to enquirers, it seems to me that no harm is done by being very careful whom we accept as such. I must own that I have not always worked on that principle, and there was a time when I was under the impression that to refuse to see a visitor, or to keep him waiting a quarter of an hour, would be to derogate from the importance of the message that I had to give, and when I would plunge without hesitation into the arguments for the Christian position with any one who asked me to do so. Possibly at the time it was the best thing to do, for it was not until I had pursued this plan that I gained any experience to enable me to discriminate; but I should certainly hesitate to advise anybody to follow my example. Unless a man professes some serious and practical reason for wanting to know why he ought to become a Christian it is not always advisable to tell him. Latterly, when I was approached on the subject of Christianity, I always replied by asking the enquirer's reasons for searching, and also by asking of what he was in search, and, if from his answer it was obvious that he was in search of something which could be found outside Christianity, I always told him so. You must remember that such a man naturally continues talking with you, generally on religious subjects, and indeed you have then the opportunity of explaining what Christianity really is, without the necessity of controversially proving its truth. He is also just as likely to return to your house as a man with whom you have entered into regular argument, and I am quite convinced that he is not less likely to appreciate Christianity at its true value than if you had allowed him to consider that any one was a proper applicant for admission into the Christian Church.

As a general rule, the thing which seems to me to succeed best with Yezdi enquirers is controversial teaching of a systematic kind. Pure controversy is sometimes necessary to remove particular objections to the Gospel message, but it has to be followed by regular instruction. On the other hand, instruction that does not bring out very clearly the contrast between Islam and Christianity is liable not to be understood. Persian enquirers seem as a rule to want help in understanding the meaning of Scripture. Several Persian converts have been brought in through the instrumentality of the Bible without the help of the missionary; but such cases are not common.

Then one of the most important points that the missionary has to bear in mind is that the Persian expects a concrete example of the Christian life. He is much more able to understand what he sees than what he simply reads, and he is anxious to know how the whole scheme works out, for he wishes to understand how much of the practical teaching of Christianity is really intended for everyday use. He is aware that in his own religion a good deal can be explained away by the mulla, and also that rather different conduct is expected from the clerical and non-clerical classes respectively. It is true that in Islam this difference is not so great as one would expect, but the Mussulman clerics as a class are certainly more particular than the laity about prayers, fasts, and attendance at the mosques. When a Persian sees the Christian colony entirely at variance with the missionary households as to religious customs and ideas, he naturally comes to the conclusion that as a Christian layman he will have to conform much more to the practice of the laity than to the practice of the clerical class, under which heading he will include all missionaries. For this reason it seems to me that it is lamentable for missionaries, clerical or otherwise, to separate themselves too much from the social life of the European colony. Work in such towns as Yezd ought to be primarily church extension, and when both missionaries and other Europeans realise this fact, and do their best to show the native that Christ is a real force in the concrete European life of the present day, the hopefulness of mission prospects becomes increased a thousandfold. But the task before the missionary is a rather more complex one, for his duty is not only to present Christ as a living force in his everyday life, but he ought also to try and avoid all conduct which he learns by experience will seem to the native not to tally with the teaching of Scripture. In other words, he must be ready to give up lawful things which he is unable to justify to those whom he is striving to teach. Such a determination will demand not only strength of purpose, but also careful and prayerful Bible study; but unless the determination is made, the work will inevitably suffer.

One unusually intelligent Behāī, who, I am glad to say, afterwards became a Christian, once brought forward an objection to Christianity, which I think is worth closely noting. He said, "You point to the comparative prosperity of Europe as an evidence of the truth of Christianity. I, who have been in India, do not doubt that Europeans have accomplished something. But it seems to me that what has been done has been done by the State organisation, which rests upon the law of retaliation, and is therefore in direct opposition to the law of Christ. Consequently these successes prove not the truth of Christianity, but rather the power of work done on exactly opposite principles." My answer, which was accepted, was to point out that although Christ in the Sermon on the Mount showed that the principle of retaliation was not to govern the actions of individual Christians, Christ's religion both as expounded by Himself before Pilate, and as presented by His apostles in the Epistles, recognises the power of the force-using governor as that of God's minister. I also pointed out that the best European State organisations had only been made possible by the Church. However, the objection was certainly one which a serious enquirer might be pardoned for advancing, and it is interesting as showing the trend of the Persian's mind when he comes into contact with European customs and Christian ideas.

There remain several difficulties, connected rather with the acceptance of converts than with the making of them. The Persian is exceedingly impulsive, and a great many enquirers who are really in earnest ask to be baptized without realising all that it will mean. This, I suppose, is a difficulty one finds everywhere. A difficulty more peculiar to Persia has already been mentioned in a previous chapter, namely, the feeling that two motives are better than one, and that the desire for earthly as well as spiritual gain only makes a man a more earnest applicant. In Yezd it is impossible to treat people who have this feeling as radically unsound, but of course they have to be taught that it is impossible to become a Christian from the two points of view, and that if they intend to make Christianity pay from the earthly point of view, they will lose the spiritual benefit. The question may perhaps be asked, how is it that in a Mohammedan country there can be supposed to be any temporal advantage in becoming a Christian? The answer to this is that the Yezdi Persian is accustomed not so much to religious as to politico-religious systems: so he regards the whole European colony with their native servants, Parsi and Mussulman, as all belonging to Christianity and under the protection of the Christian authorities, and this idea is very largely kept up by the servants themselves. Servants in a Christian household will almost invariably join in any form of Christian worship, and it would be impossible to explain to them that they did not to some extent participate in the spiritual advantages of Christianity. They recognise, however, a distinct difference between taking service and accepting baptism. Probably in their heart of hearts they believe that taking service is temporary, and accepting baptism permanent. Amongst people who are accustomed to a view of the household largely corresponding to the patriarchal view, such notions cannot be altogether eradicated. So enquirers, when they first ask for baptism, do not necessarily see the enormous danger, but only realise that they will be brought into close touch with a community that seems to them to include other natives who wear the same dress as themselves. Of course when the enquirers are junior members of strict Mussulman households, or in other equally unfavourable circumstances, they realise that their peril will be extreme; but heads of households sometimes expect much less danger. Then again, the Mussulman is accustomed to secret religions, for *taqiya*, the denial of faith in times of danger, has always been considered lawful by Shiahs, and it is used by the Babis. Although the enquirer learns at a very early date that such conduct is regarded by the Christian as sin, it takes him some time to realise the exact degree to which his Christianity is likely to be public. Lastly, although he may be told that converts are not under consular protection, in a country where law means so little and custom so much he is not likely to understand how real are the boundaries of treaty rights. This will perhaps give some idea of the amount of misapprehension, both as to the meaning of Christianity and also as to the danger of accepting it, which may possibly exist after a considerable amount of talk and enquiry; nor would the dangers of embracing Christianity be made altogether obvious by a single riot or martyrdom; for the whole operation of Persian law, or want of law, is irregular and spasmodic, and in a town like Yezd things which are foolhardy in January are often attended with no more than ordinary risk in June.

Under these circumstances the question of the admission of professing converts to baptism must necessarily be extremely difficult. In towns where the mission work is in a pioneering stage it has to be primarily settled by the European missionary; and not until the difficulty has been by him sufficiently solved to admit of the foundation of a church, can much of this burden be placed upon other shoulders. Sometimes he may have the good fortune to have among his earlier converts a wholly trustworthy man, who, from his greater experience of native character and knowledge of what is going on in the town, can advise and counsel him, but even then the main responsibility must rest with the European. The difficulty is greatly enhanced by the fact that the missionary in Persia does not really live amongst the people, and that the clerical missionary usually sees enquirers only in his own house. Under these circumstances it is perhaps well not to apply too many tests, for it is not easy to get a test which is really sound. One test which is sometimes advocated is the practice of keeping the catechumen waiting for a long period; but the result of this is frequently to deter those who are weakly in earnest, whereas a Persian who has a worldly end to serve is capable of extraordinary patience. It is sometimes urged that an unsound convert brings the whole band of native Christians and enquirers into extreme danger; but I am inclined to think that, in the circumstances of our pioneer missions as they at present exist, a totally unsound catechumen may do almost as much harm as even an unsound convert. It is hard to avoid the conclusion that the only way to deal with the situation is to baptize all persons who after full instruction, not too hurriedly given, profess conversion and demand baptism, and even after baptism to observe a certain degree of caution towards the newly baptized. If it is absolutely proved that such converts are behaving in a manner that is not only weak but actively hostile towards Christ's cause, they must be excommunicated; but the most necessary point of all is that as much attention should be paid to the instruction of converts as to the instruction of catechumens. It is of course impossible to expect that all points of character should be absolutely changed after baptism, and nobody ought to be cut loose from the Church in a place like Yezd, unless he is actively hostile; and, even when actual hostility has been proved, an opportunity ought to be given for the man's return.

As to the advisability of giving converts material help, a great deal may be said against it in theory, but in practice it is at times absolutely necessary. After all, it is impossible to avoid mistakes, and the attempt to avoid all mistakes in detail is only too likely to lead to the more general one of entirely failing to present Christ in any form whatsoever.

The conclusions which have been stated in this chapter are not intended to be taken as the fully thought out summing up of an extremely complex and difficult problem. They are the result of rather less than six years' experience of the mission-field. But just as there is a value in first impressions of country, so there is a value in first impressions of difficulties in work. At five and a half years first impressions of country have passed away, and consequently the contents of the earlier chapters of this book, which deal with country and surroundings, can hardly be so characterised; but at this period the difficulties of mission work are only just beginning to spread themselves out before one's eyes. So when we pass from country to character, from character to opportunity, and from opportunity to suggestion, we pass from subjects with which it is comparatively easy to become familiar to subjects which need life-long and careful study. I have tried in writing this chapter to eliminate from the style that consciousness of uncertainty which is frequently so irritating to the reader; but in doing this I should explain that I am fully conscious of the superficial nature of much that I have written. At the same time, the view that I have gained of mission work in Yezd is a full one compared with that which is possible for people at a distance, and for that reason it may be considered worth stating.

A VIEW OF YEZD.

CHAPTER VII

In Persia the missionary has no right to teach and preach in public places. He cannot take up his stand in the bazaars and proclaim the Gospel. He can talk to the people who come to his house, and to a certain extent he can talk with crowds in open caravanserais or in the villages, but anything approximating to public teaching is only done on sufferance, and without any established licence. So the ordinary evangelistic missionary's first task is to get on terms of social intercourse with a sufficiently large number of natives to afford him a field for work. Afterwards he may arrange for services, either in his own house or in the house of some other European, and so his visitors will become congregations and his talks sermons.

Now, although it is obvious that such work can only be carried on when it is acceptable to the natives, the work may be accepted for very various reasons. If the missionary knows enough of the Persian language, of native ideas, and above all of the message he has come to deliver, he will, in a town like Yezd, without the help of school or medical work, attract a large number of people to his house. In Persia there is just now a great seeking after truth, which, though due in part to traceable causes, seems in its entirety to be simply one of those mysterious movements which God evokes at certain seasons in all lands for the furtherance of His Kingdom. One class attracted by such a man as I have described would therefore be real enquirers, and with them would be mixed a second class of people who have been called religious sightseers. These men though not apparently so good a field for work as the first class, would still, if properly handled and directed, prove a perfectly possible sphere for serious missionary operations. So also would the third class of callers, who would be men not primarily interested in religious questions at all, but who would nevertheless follow the fashion of calling on the newly-arrived foreigner, and would be generally willing to follow any line of conversation that was agreeable to their host. Of course a man who did not intend to engage in school or medical work would naturally be careful to take full advantage of such contacts as these, and of others that he would naturally make from time to time; he would order his life in such a way as to get day by day into close touch with the people of the town; and he would equip himself with a material outfit that would enable him to exchange courtesies with natives of various classes. I am not speaking of a man who elected to spend most of his time itinerating in the villages: of such work as this I have little experience: but I am convinced that a stationary missionary, fairly well equipped at all points, does not in a town like Yezd absolutely need the help of more elaborate aids to enable him to get into touch with his work. To suppose this is to ignore the extraordinary preparation which God has made in Persia for the preaching of the Gospel.

Before passing on to the very real demand for missionaries of a somewhat different kind, it will be well to mention some points connected with the life of the European missionary in the country. There are probably very few men or women at present working in Persia, who have not at the outset of their work felt doubtful whether the details of their household life could not be simplified, so as to bring them into closer touch with the poorer part of the population. It is hardly possible to write a serious book on missionary conditions without expressing an opinion on this question. There is, I think, no doubt that it is a great mistake for a missionary in Persia to be known as one who is leading the life of a wealthy man. It is considered by many of the enquirers to be absolutely inconsistent with Christianity, and I am not sure that this judgment is incorrect. Temporary advantages might sometimes be gained by such a reputation, but in the end the work would suffer.

Generally speaking, however, it is the habit of missionaries in the Persian stations to live as economically as is compatible with European style, so far as their strictly personal expenses are concerned. Many things which appear at first sight to be luxurious prove on closer acquaintance to be mere substitutes for the ordinary necessaries of the simplest English life. Other things prove to be absolutely essential to health in a hot climate, while yet another class are not exactly necessary, but they are comforts of the cheapest kind. People who are economising seriously in Eastern lands have to put up with so much that is really difficult that they make a great mistake if they unnecessarily deny themselves small things which can be had for the asking, simply because they have regarded such things as luxuries in England. But although the existence of careful economies on European lines may be sufficient to prevent an intelligent enquirer from thinking that the missionary is untrue to his creed, such economies can never bring the missionary into touch with the poor of the East in the same way that living in a model lodging-house might under some circumstances bring a home clergyman into close touch with the English poor. The real analogy would be for the missionary to live as an Eastern dervish, or as a native of the artisan class, and although this might be sometimes helpful and advisable, the principle of its general advisability could not be accepted. To begin with, it would be only possible for a bachelor, and, in a country where no man can possibly give individual instruction to women, the bachelor is at a great disadvantage. Secondly, it must not be forgotten that, although the missionary living the life of an European has been accepted in Persia, the missionary wearing Persian dress and living like a native has not yet been accepted, and would probably find himself not only at variance with the consular authorities but also regarded with a great deal of suspicion by the natives themselves. In a matter of this kind it is impossible to ignore apostolic precedent, and one thing that cannot but strike the student of the missionary methods of the period covered by the Acts of the Apostles is that the apostles generally, and notably St Paul, seem never to have adopted a method of missionary work which would have seemed to the inhabitants of the district to be *outré*, when some more natural method of work was equally possible. Nothing would strike the Persian as more *outré* than for the ordinary European to drop the form of life which is expected of the Ferangi, and to adopt the manners and customs of the native of Persia, particularly as he would probably have to periodically re-assume European clothes. If he was going to work among the Mussulmans as a Christian missionary, I suppose he would have to choose between life as an Armenian and life as a Mussulman. Life as an Armenian would have this advantage over the other, that he would not be supposed to be hiding his religion. But the life of the Armenian in a town like Yezd is the life of a stranger in a foreign town, and would not bring the missionary into very much closer touch with the Mussulmans than life as a European. By assuming the dress and manners of an Armenian of any class whatsoever, one would simply forfeit the respect that is usually paid by the Persian to the Ferangi, without gaining anything that could not have been gained by other and more ordinary methods. On the other hand, life as a Mussulman would be attended with serious difficulties. In a town where there was a Ferangi colony wearing European dress, such a man would very possibly be regarded as a soldier is regarded who attempts to mix with the enemy without his uniform. I can conceive circumstances which might make an experiment of this kind worth trying, but it would be madness for any one to attempt it for missionary purposes, who had not extraordinary experience of the country and a full mastery over the language.

I think then we must take it for granted that the kind of life which missionaries are living in Persia at the present time will have to be accepted, with such modifications as future events and further experience may suggest, as the normal method for Europeans who wish to carry on missionary work in the country. There are one or two tasks which lie before the pioneer missionary which seem to be made more easy by the possession of an ordinary European household. First of all, he has to be prepared to work amongst the European colony. Secondly, it is well for him to possess sufficient influence and standing in the town to be able to help the converts or enquirers in time of trouble. Thirdly, he wants to be in touch with all classes of natives, and this would probably only be possible for a man who stood in the highest rank as a native, or for one who stood outside native rank altogether.

Every missionary has to do a good deal of visiting. All visits have not got to be returned, but a certain number must be. It is well not to return all visits, for otherwise it is difficult to get secret enquirers to come to your house, or people who are too poor to receive you in their own houses. The usual Persian habit is never to pay a visit without first of all asking leave, but though this rule has to be observed towards others, it is best to make it clear that your own house is an office, and only to insist on notice for visits of civility when they are made by people who are likely to prove awkward. Paying visits to Persian houses has a certain value to the missionary, as it introduces him to Persian life and manners, and puts him on easier terms with the natives, but it seldom affords the evangelistic missionary who is working amongst men his best opportunity for direct missionary work. There is too much publicity, and too many interruptions. The best missionary work is usually done on one's own premises; and in Yezd I have known enquirers and visitors begin coming at six o'clock in the morning, and go on almost without intermission till ten o'clock at night; but at that time I was connected with scholastic work, which, although requiring only superintendence, advertised my presence in the town to a considerable degree. One of the things that is therefore most necessary in a place like Yezd for the evangelistic missionary is an absolutely well-ordered household. Everything ought to go by clockwork. Almost every visitor has to be treated as an ordinary social guest, and unless the arrangements are nearly perfect, either his attention or the missionary's will be called away from the conversation. A missionary in such a position ought to pay close attention to the number and description of his tea-cups and pipes. One class of visitors ought to be properly served with silver-mounted hookahs and three tiny cups of very hot tea, brought in at intervals of ten minutes, and this without any previous notice to the servant. Another class of visitor ought to have a European cup of tea holding about three times as much as the Persian cup, and a box of cigarettes, so that he and his host may be able to talk without further interruption till the end of the interview. A third class of visitor, who has given notice, ought to be prepared for beforehand, and served with iced sherbet. Then again, a decision has to be made according to the status of the guest as to whether the missionary shall be served with tea at the same time or not. All this requires the most careful training of servants, and any inattention to detail may produce an atmosphere which makes teaching exceedingly difficult. Further, the servants have to know who should be shown into a private room, and who can be allowed to mix with other guests. These are just a few of the minor points which are nevertheless of real importance. To come to points which are obviously more serious. Servants have to be procured who can act with firmness when people attempt to take liberties, and who are at the same time absolutely civil. Servants in a Christian household have to be good-tempered; and in order to effect this they have to be kept well occupied without being overworked, in a house where the chief work is meeting emergencies. They have to be taught some consistent and systematic line that is to be observed in dealing with the countless beggars who every day come to your house. They have to be rendered as truthful as possible in every matter connected with the missionary's business. They have to be paid a rate of wages which will make honesty and contentment possible, and which will neither spoil the market, nor be incompatible with reasonable economy. It is needless to say very much more about these matters; sufficient has already been said to make it plain that the problem of household arrangement is an exceedingly difficult one, particularly as the servants sleep in their own houses at a distance, all but one, who stays for the night; and they generally expect to go home for their mid-day meal. My own impression is that as the evangelistic missionary's house is almost his parish, he may be excused if he thinks right to expend a very great deal of time over its arrangements, and to consider this just as much missionary work as the teaching of enquirers. If the missionary intends to aim at anything that is likely to be satisfactory in this matter, he certainly needs an enormous degree of faith, and will do well to make his efforts in this direction the subject of very earnest prayer.

SCENES OF YEZDI LIFE.

The centre of these three pictures represents two men smoking opium. Behind them is a *qalian*, or hookah, for tobacco; in front is a sherbet bowl, and also a small tea-table with sweets underneath.

The picture on the left represents two men; one holding a rosary, and the other holding a hookah.

The single figure on the right is a Jew, with his book for divining. The Persians use the Jews as diviners a good deal.

Another difficulty in seeing enquirers in the house is the arrangement of times. Missionaries are sometimes blamed for not sufficiently consorting with Europeans in the ordinary amusements of the colony, but there is one great difficulty about this. The times when you naturally take exercise in the East are the times when the native artisan or shopkeeper is off work. Supposing that the evangelistic missionary is seldom at home at such times as these, the more industrious Persians get to regard him as inaccessible, and his enquirers begin to consist of people who for some reason or other have very little to do. It is hardly necessary to enter into the difficulties that may follow.

We have been hitherto speaking only of directly evangelistic methods of missionary work; but almost all missionaries have something to do with philanthropic work also. These philanthropic efforts are not solely undertaken as means to an end. In most cases they are treated as an end in themselves by the missionary, and generally speaking they are things which could not well be left undone. Medical missionaries will tell you that their standing orders are to heal the sick and preach the Gospel; but I think we may say very much more generally that the presentation of the Gospel without adequate and proportionate care for the minds and bodies of those surrounding us, would be impossible. For the Gospel is the message of our Saviour, and any message that was so delivered would entirely fail to represent that Saviour's attitude. I doubt whether any one would call in question this aspect of the case, but when we come to discuss how much philanthropic work is really necessary, we are face to face with a difficult problem. In matters like this the decision must depend not only upon the needs of the people with whom the missionaries are brought in contact, but also upon the nature of the church or congregation of Christians that supports them, and whose material as well as spiritual force they are appointed to convey to the mission field. There is a great difference between the position of a band of men sent out by an infinitesimal body of earnest Christians who have the greatest difficulty in subscribing the means of their support, and that of a band sent out by an exceedingly wealthy Christian church.

Present-day missionaries sent out by the Church Missionary Society have passed outside the conditions of the first class, but they cannot be said to fully belong to the second. They are supported by a large number of people, but those who give most are generally those whose purses are least elastic. In the countries to which they go they are treated with the greatest courtesy by British officials, and accepted as representatives of the religion of England by their fellow-countrymen. Naturally the native expects more from them than they are really able to give, and this increases the difficulty when they have to decide what they are bound to do as ministers of Christ and as representatives of those who send them, for the people committed to their charge. Naturally, and I think rightly, they do not wholly shut their eyes to the attitude and expectations of the natives. But, unfortunately, the Persians think that there ought to be no difficulty about anything. The average native cannot get out of his head the idea that we are sent by the Government, or, if not by the Government, by the whole nation under its religious authorities. Those who know anything of English thought and feeling realise that foreign missions are now well established in the popular regard in England, and many Yezdis have a confused notion that in our country education, medical attendance, and support in old age are free to everybody, irrespective of class, and that as Christians we are all anxious to extend this system as far as we can to other nations. Of course views like this are variable, but it may be seen after a moment's consideration that in a country where the need for schools, for hospitals, and sometimes for relief is very real, and where the native is capable of believing such absurdities about the European as have been stated, if the missionary does not to a large extent take up the white man's burden, he is likely to lose any influence which God may have given him. Consequently I think we may say that the philanthropic work of missionaries in Persia must not only be regarded as a means to evangelisation, although this is an aspect which must largely determine its importance. Primarily it is a spiritual necessity created by three things, the comparative wealth of the Christians who send out the missionaries, the comparative poverty of the natives who are ready to be relieved, and the obvious commandment of Almighty God.

Philanthropic work in Yezd is of three kinds; medical work, school work, and the work of poor relief. The last is of course not recognised or supported by the Church Missionary Society. It is not within the scope of this book to deal with either of these three provinces of work in detail. All that I wish at present to explain is the way in which they seem to strike the Persian mind, and contribute to the general campaign of the mission.

Relief work is of all the three most absolutely necessitated by the essential difference between the circumstances of the missionary and his supporters on the one hand, and those of a certain section of the natives on the other. But from an evangelistic standpoint it is the least directly productive in effect; so we have never in Yezd used for this purpose any funds not specially subscribed for it, and such money has been collected almost entirely from the resident Europeans. There is a very great deal of terrible poverty in Persia which is not touched by the native charities. In Yezd, particularly towards the end of our stay in the town, things were in a very bad way. Yezd is really an industrial town, and not less than half of the grain supply comes from outside, chiefly from the Shiraz district. Most of the people are silk weavers. The silkworms used to be reared in the Yezd district, but the extreme droughts rendered this source of supply very insecure, and after the great famine that occurred some years ago there were not sufficient trees left for the business to be continued in this way. Cocoons were then brought from Rasht, and this system proved more satisfactory till lately, when the Rasht cocoons were diverted to France and Italy. The natural result was a great deal of poverty in Yezd, which was most felt among the poor Jews, who since the famine year have had no looms but have devoted themselves to winding and spinning the silk. Then again, after the Babi massacre of 1903, something had to be done for the large number of widows and orphans. In this work the Europeans were by no means alone, for the sufferers were helped both by the Babi merchants and also by a large number of the Parsis. The Parsis are generally very good in looking after their own poor, but the Mussulmans give money so indiscriminately that their charities cause more poverty than they relieve. Although the work of poor relief is not as a rule the direct means of bringing in converts, it helps the evangelistic work enormously by saving valuable time. Before it could be organised the number of begging enquirers who had the very smallest interest, if any, in the Gospel message, was so large as to seriously impede more important work. It is much easier and better to keep the two things more separate, and to be able to say to a man, "If you want to read with me, well and good, but if you want material help, then you must do so and so." This does not necessarily mean that the man who is relieved gets no chance of hearing the Gospel. The Jews, who came in a body, used always to have a chapter of the Gospel read to them by my mirza, and any man who showed a disposition to come as a real enquirer after his case had been looked into and relieved was thoroughly welcomed. But the practice of trying to earn a *kran* by wasting hours of the missionary's time was effectually discouraged.

I think also that the practice of separating poor relief as much as possible from the work with enquirers helps to explain to the native our view of the Christian Church. That some explanation is necessary is undoubted. During a severe famine in Kirman, over two hundred respectable Mussulmans, chiefly shopkeepers, came into the courtyard of the Consulate, and wanted to take protection under the British flag. Major Phillott was then Consul, and they explained to him that the price of bread was so prohibitive that they could not live any longer under the regulations of the Persian officials. Their leader was a Seyid. Major Phillott tried to explain that, although he sympathised with them greatly, he could do nothing for them unless it was to give them pecuniary help. He offered them a hundred *krans*, but they explained that they were not beggars. They further said that they were quite ready to become Christians if they could only get cheap bread. The end of the whole business was that the Consul paid an unofficial visit to the Governor, and got him to promise that bread should be lowered to a more or less normal price by gradual reductions spread over a period of ten days. It is easy to understand that people who could go to a Consul in a famine and ask to be accepted as Christians in order to be able to buy bread at a fair price, thinking I suppose that Consular pressure would then be brought to bear upon the Governor on their behalf, might easily get an absolutely wrong notion of what was going on, if circumstances forced the missionary whose general business was seeing enquirers to use funds for poor relief without carefully separating these two branches of work. Even the practice of giving occasional relief to very poor enquirers from one's own purse is liable to great misinterpretation and abuse. Men will frequently come to you and ask for support, so as to enable them to leave their ordinary trades and listen to your teaching. Myself, I think that there are occasions when poor people have come from a distance and are certainly interested, where something of this kind has to be done, the man if possible being made to work for his money; but it is easy to see how extremely dangerous it would be to encourage expectations, and how easily natives might get the idea that enquiry, and still more Christianity, entitled them to payment. Consequently, even if it could not be demonstrated that an actual saving of time was effected by making of poor relief a distinct organisation, there would be still a very great deal to be said for the practice.

To administer poor relief in a town like Yezd on anything approaching to a sound system necessitates a great deal of reliance upon native information, and also a certain amount of high-handed dealing. Any food or clothing given must be of a class only acceptable to the very poorest, for otherwise the candidates for relief would be too numerous to deal with in even the roughest fashion. These considerations will explain two things; first of all it will be readily understood that it is much easier to give systematic relief to members of a native community which is more or less down-trodden, such as the Jews or Babis; for although a certain number of mistakes will be made in dealing with these peoples, they will be much less resented, and will militate much less against the success of the whole effort. Secondly, it will be obvious that such relief will not call forth very much gratitude from the recipients. The very fact of investigation gives the idea to the Persian mind that charity is given grudgingly. Also it is impossible to handle a hundred screaming women in a small compound without a certain amount of what appears to be stern dealing, and after all in most instances the relief given is not as much as we ourselves would like it to be. Added to this, most of the people receiving relief are under the impression that we are simply dispensing a small part of the large supplies sent to us for the purpose from abroad; and the Jews, of whom nearly a hundred families were receiving relief in Yezd last winter, believed that all that was given to them came from their co-religionists in Europe. The Babis of course looked upon the matter rather differently, but people who hold the theory of *savabs* in the way in which Persians do, have always a feeling that anything given to them means one for them and two for the giver. At the same time Persians who are interested in Christianity, and who are not themselves candidates for poor relief, see a great deal more in the system than do those who are more intimately concerned with it. They often understand that the willingness to take trouble in localising need, and the absolute recklessness with which we incur as many curses as blessings in the performance of our work, points to an utterly different ideal from that which is accepted in Islam; and whether they are prepared to approve it or not, anything which shows the native part of the fundamental distinction between Islam and Christianity must in the end be of enormous assistance in missionary work.

School work in Yezd is very greatly appreciated by a somewhat limited class, but it means continual friction. The whole Mussulman clerical class as a body are keenly opposed to it. More curiously it aroused the greatest opposition from a small but not unimportant section of the Parsis. The Parsis are a puzzling people. For though they are strong, intelligent, thrifty, industrious, grateful, and comparatively honest, they seem to have a tendency to produce in their community a sufficient number of exceptionally disagreeable specimens of humanity to greatly check their natural progress. I myself believe that this is due to the prevalence of agnosticism amongst them, but, however that may be, the result is that the Yezd community is always pestered by internal intrigues. I do not think that the opposition to my school was religious, for the *dastūrs*, that is the Zoroastrian priests, were always very friendly. I have always put it down rather to internal intrigue.

My school work was originally undertaken at the explicit request of the natives, and the boys came chiefly, but not wholly, from the upper classes. It would be difficult, and very questionably advisable, to start school work in a town like Yezd except under pressure from the natives. Even when the work has been forced on one, it is very difficult to maintain it. Not only is there still opposition from such quarters as I have mentioned, but it is only with the greatest difficulty that competent native assistance can be secured. If native assistance cannot be secured, the missionary who has work with enquirers will have difficulty in finding time even for short classes. Short classes may be the best thing under certain circumstances, but in a town like Yezd they do not meet the whole need. Boys are brought to you in Persia in most cases primarily to be taught English, but this demand for English is not the only requirement, nor is it the only need that is felt by the Persians. Persians will frequently tell you that they bring their boys to you for education in the largest sense; but we made it a practice in Yezd only to accept boys who wished to learn English, and whose parents could show that the knowledge of English was likely to be of some use to them. Very frequently poor lads would come, under the impression that the town was going to be occupied by Europeans, and that all who had learnt English would get remunerative employment in Yezd. The only thing to do under such circumstances was to explain the true state of affairs, and then to insist on payment being made in advance for all books, and also upon the payment of a six months' fee. The first argument was generally rather ineffectual, but supported by the second it always had the desired result. If it could be shown that a poor boy was likely to reap advantage from a knowledge of English, fees were always remitted, and in some cases books were provided.

The ordinary fees were very small, but had to be paid in advance for the half year. The education given comprised Persian subjects, arithmetic, English, and elementary geography. The Bible was read in Persian, night and morning, and the boys were expected to be present during the Bible reading and prayers. Latterly the whole routine work was put into the hands of natives, but I paid as much attention not only to superintendence but also to conversational classes as my other engagements would allow. Naturally there was a great difference in the efficiency of the school at different times. At first it was with the greatest difficulty that the work could be carried on at all, and what I was able to do was of the most trivial character. In the end, owing to the excellent work done by my Armenian assistants, and by Mihraban, my Parsi mirza, the results were really excellent. On the whole, I think I may say that the confidence reposed in the school system by the natives, was greater than I could have expected, and in many things both boys and parents proved excessively forbearing.

THE SCHOOL.

This was drawn when the school was quite small.

The figure on the left sitting in a chair is Mesak, my first Armenian schoolmaster. I am on the right leaning against a desk. The thing in

my hand is a pointer and not an instrument of punishment. There
is a wall in front of me on which was hung the thing to which I was
pointing. I should perhaps mention that the square fire-place coming
forward into the room is not of a usual shape: fire-places are generally
let into the wall. All the boys in this picture are Mussulmans.

In the matter of gratitude they showed discrimination, but the gratitude
that was shown me by the pupils who stuck to the school for any time, and
by their parents, was extraordinary. The lads themselves, both Parsi and
Mussulman, were on the whole intelligent and teachable. I had, however,
very much greater success in dealing with them when I had not myself
to undertake the routine work of the schoolmaster. Possibly this was due
partially to my not being suited for such work, but I am inclined to think
that in most cases elementary school work is not quite the proper field
for the European missionary in Persia. There is perhaps no harm in the
evangelistic missionary who has not yet perfected himself in the language
devoting more of his time to it; but, considering the enormous value of the
work from a spiritual point of view, there should be no difficulty in getting
funds to employ extra native assistants where the European missionary
feels himself in a position to organise and superintend a school for native
boys. These remarks do not apply to schools for girls, for which properly
qualified native teachers can only be found with the greatest difficulty. My
feeling is that not only can the fully qualified European missionary be more
usefully employed if his time is not too largely given up to school work,
but also much of the actual work of the school is better done by natives
under European management, and the influence of the missionary with the
boys may be rather increased than checked by his not having to teach them
their ordinary lessons. It is, however, very difficult to separate what may be
taken as a general principle in Persia from what was true of our particular
circumstances in Yezd. I have before mentioned that I do not consider
myself very fitted for ordinary school work.

In the boys' school in Yezd we had at first a custom of never admitting a
child until his father had been seen, and had thoroughly understood to what
extent he would receive religious teaching. I used to pledge myself to teach
nothing to the boy of Christian tradition apart from what could be found in
the *Kalāmu'llah*, that is, the Word of God accepted by the Mohammedans,
an expression which was thoroughly understood to include the whole
of the Christian Bible. This may seem at first sight to have been merely a
quibble, but it must not be forgotten in dealing with the Mussulman, that
he is afraid of something like Romanism which will stand out in political
as well as religious rivalry to Islam, and that he knows very little of the
special tenets of Protestants. My assurance would at least have satisfied him

that no attempt would be made to draw the boy into a foreign politico-religious system. The fathers were also told that the boys would be expected to attend prayers. Latterly, as the school and its methods got better known, the necessity for these precautions disappeared. However, when boys at the school came to me, as they frequently did, and told me that they wished to know more about Christianity, I invariably insisted that their fathers or guardians should be informed before they received special instruction. Of course they were always free to come to the Sunday School, which was held for them by my Armenian assistant, and which was attended by a few boys from other schools as well, and occasionally by one or two men. Many of the boys also were extremely regular in their attendance at the services, which we held at first in our houses, and afterwards in a chapel which was built in the hospital.

Our school work in Yezd was in every way a thoroughly effective evangelistic agency. It brought me into touch with scores of adults who without it would never have entered my house. By increasing the general business with which I was surrounded, it also greatly facilitated my contact with those who came to me as regular enquirers. All this was additional to the direct effects of the school work, which I have reason to believe were exceedingly satisfactory. Altogether school work proved in Yezd to be one of the most effective forms of missionary effort.

At the same time one or two things have to be borne in mind about it. First of all, it is extremely difficult for the evangelistic missionary to organise school work for the teaching of Persian subjects only that will successfully compete with the native schools. Further, the need for such work is not greatly felt by the natives. But the teaching of English is one of those things which missionaries are distinctly asked to undertake, and which they are able to undertake with great advantage. In a short time I have no doubt that industrial education will be an even more pressing need. The argument for schools as against classes is that their effect upon the moral character of the boys is much greater, and that the qualified missionary has by himself time for neither, unless indeed the classes are to be very short ones, and the staff that would be needed to properly undertake classes might just as well manage a school.

With regard to fees, it seems to me that when assistants are employed fees should be charged; but to get fees that would really cover the expenses would be impossible, and I personally think that the lower the fee the more easy it is to enforce its payment, and to keep the arrangements of the school entirely in one's own hands. This, however, is a matter over which there is plenty of room for difference of opinion. Of one thing I am certain, and that is that in the up-country towns educational work must begin amongst classes who can support the missionary against Persian intrigues and the direct opposition of the Mulla class. In starting a school in a Mussulman country the object of the missionary must always be to get the establishment regarded as a settled fact, consequently certain things which would otherwise be unimportant become matters of extreme moment. For instance, if anything should happen to the teaching staff, the school must be kept running, even if the pupils cannot under the circumstances make great progress. At one time I had to keep the school going when I was myself laid up in a sick room, and had no assistant capable of teaching much more than the primers. The day's work for the first class was written out by my wife, and sent into the school by a servant. However, the school survived, and some while later, when it was again properly staffed, we saw the effects of our persistence, for while the town was absolutely under mob law, the school was never without a certain number of boys attending at the regular hours. Again, when the position of the school is temporarily assured, nothing can be better than some sort of public Speech Day, which both advertises its existence, and makes people understand that you regard its permanence as a matter of course. The fact is that in Persia all opposition and persecution is spasmodic, and if you can manage to go your own way for a sufficient time and then take your position for granted, you will be allowed to do things which vastly exceed your recognised rights and liberties.

Medical mission work in Persia has been described by those who have been actively engaged in it. Under these circumstances I intend to speak very much less about it than I have done about other methods of work, though it is at least as important as any. It would be possible to divide the provinces of medical work in several ways, but it seems to me to be best treated under three heads: hospital work, dispensary work, and medical visiting. The branch of medical work which is most obviously necessary, and also perhaps least productive of direct spiritual results is the work of the dispensary. A doctor settled in a Persian town is primarily expected to see all comers and to provide them with medicines. Indeed the Persian will come to the European for treatment whether he is a doctor or not. The business of the dispensary affords an excellent opportunity for giving an address on religious subjects, but comparatively little for systematic teaching of individuals, though contacts may be made during dispensary hours that may lead to further enquiry, and of course even systematic teaching can be given during dispensary hours by a determined worker.

Medical visiting is just what the missionary is able to make it. The over-worked doctor with more visits than he can pay in the day has to be content with a very occasional reading and a word here and there as opportunity offers; but there is no doubt that the opportunity is unique, and if time can be made during medical visits for more systematic spiritual teaching, such teaching is likely for several reasons to carry exceptional weight. Although perhaps medical visits give a better opportunity to the doctor who wishes to himself follow up the work with religious teaching, dispensary work affords a much better opportunity for the bringing of other evangelists into such touch with the patients as will make it possible to find out any serious enquirers and to rouse others to further interest. The great difficulty in dispensary work and medical visiting, regarded as evangelistic agencies in Persia, is that the number of contacts is almost too large to handle. To begin with, the staff of missionaries is inadequate, and the difficulty is further increased by the peculiarities of the Persian, who in most cases is almost untouched by any teaching that is not systematic, and that does not go somewhat deeply into fundamentals. Of course these kinds of medical work produce more contacts than does anything else, but the difficulty in Persia is not to bring people within the hearing of the Gospels, but to convey to them something of the meaning of the Gospel. What makes the medical mission of the present time in Persia all-important is not that it is absolutely necessary for the purpose of bringing the evangelist into touch with the native, though in certain times and places it may be still greatly needed for this purpose; but the great point is that it has often explained the meaning of Christ crucified to men and women who without it seemed unable to grasp the Christian idea. This I believe to be true of all branches of medical mission work that I have mentioned, but at the same time it must be owned that the branch which has hitherto proved most satisfactory as a direct evangelistic agency is that connected with the hospital. Nobody can speak too highly of the potentialities of hospital work in Persia. It is almost inconceivable what misunderstanding of the doctor's attitude is possible in out-patient work in a Mussulman country. He is a bad man trying to work off his sins. He is sent out by the English Government at a high salary. He is making a very good profit out of the work. He is an instance of the subjection of the infidel to the Mussulman by the power of God. All these notions gradually die away under the systematic life and discipline of the hospital, with its atmosphere of trust and repose. Day by day men meet the doctor and his assistants and learn to know them; they see the quiet persistence of their kindness, and its penetration into the smallest detail; best of all, they hear the Word of God day by day brought into a connected story and an intelligible system of salvation. In the best conducted hospitals the only misconception that is likely to remain is the belief that the missionaries as a body are trying to win a high place in Heaven by *savabs*. This dies very hard, and all we can say is that the hospital system, perhaps partly by its more definite discipline, tends to eradicate it. It is true that some workers have produced similar results by importing the atmosphere of Christian hospital work into the medical visit or the dispensary; but the point to be noted is that what is natural in the Christian hospital has in other forms of medical work to be deliberately and persistently fostered. In these if the highest spiritual results are to be obtained, there must be on the part of the worker a determination rather to guide the organisation towards them, than to depend on its essential qualities as a missionary force. It is not that hospital equipment is an essential for a doctor who wants to preach the Gospel, but no matter what a missionary may be, clergyman, lay evangelist, or medical, it is only by getting into close touch with the native, and by systematic and persevering teaching, that he can expect to extend Christ's Kingdom in Persian towns.

Of course the position of the medical missionary who is invited to the town by those in authority, as is frequently the case, is very different from that of most other missionaries. There may be a real demand for school teaching, but even when school work has been started and placed on a satisfactory footing, it never appeals so generally to the interest of all classes as to be superior to any intrigue that may arise, or to bursts of fanatical bigotry. At the same time the medical missionary who has gone to a new station finds that even when invited he is on trial. When free medicines are given, as on some occasions they have been for a short period, two-thirds of the people throw them away without using them. Even those who have invited him are quite ready to turn against him, at any rate behind his back. These difficulties, although real, are minor ones, and there are very few European doctors, possessed of an ordinary amount of common-sense and a good material equipment, who cannot get over them in a short while. The real danger is lest the missionary by regarding these difficulties as more serious than they really are should become too absorbed in his efforts to overcome them. Medical work is really an enormous power. It may make possible, under God's providence, steps and measures which would otherwise be utterly impossible. But if it is to be fully used to God's glory, these God-given powers must be realised, and put forth to their full extent.

Medical and school work have one other advantage besides those that have been mentioned, for they enable a class of men to participate in mission work who as ordinary evangelistic missionaries would be useless. In the first place, there is the newly-arrived European, who imperfectly understands the language, and who yet may do more or less effective work while he is still studying, if he is connected with a medical or educational organisation. Secondly, if it were not for schools and medical work it would be exceedingly difficult for the Persian missions to employ natives, except in menial capacities or in positions attended with the gravest peril. Here to my mind we have one of the greatest arguments for medical and school work, and this from the directly evangelistic standpoint.

This brings the subject of methods of work in Persian towns like Yezd to a conclusion. It is not impossible to work as a simple evangelist, but it needs certain qualifications and abilities. Generally speaking, the ordinary missionary must be prepared to use both hands and both feet, and to enter in whatever way seems most expedient into the life of the town. There is no room for university work, and technical instruction has not yet been tried, but elementary school work and medical work are both much needed and much appreciated, and they further afford an abundant field for directly evangelistic labour.

CONCLUSION

We have now seen something not only of the Yezdi's life, of his character, and of his mental attitude towards the missionary, but also something of the way in which the modern missionary attempts to meet this attitude. Of course it cannot be claimed that the estimate of the Yezdi's position that has been made in these pages is in any way final, or that it is one with which all acquainted with the subject would certainly concur. To have limited myself to the greatest common measure of opinion on such a matter would have prevented me altogether from touching on many questions, and would have left me very little to say on others. As the book stands, I can claim that it is truthful in matters of fact, and in other things sufficiently sound to form a basis for other people's corrections; and as many find it less easy to state their own views than to combat those of other persons, I am not without hopes that it may be useful, even if my conclusions should prove altogether unacceptable. Also it may be pointed out that, though I have throughout spoken of the Yezdi and of Yezd, these have been taken as special instances of a Persian and his town. Other places in central Persia may differ in particulars, but there will in most cases be a general similarity.

Perhaps a short summary of the points which have been noted in the preceding pages may not be without value. We have seen first of all the strange staccato effect of Persian scenery, particularly of that which meets the eye of the Yezdi, and have noticed how this has influenced the Yezdi's mind. Then we have seen the extreme insularity of the town, and how this has given rise to symptoms which resemble intense fanatical bigotry, but on the other hand how this insularity may be utilised by the foreigner when it is once understood. Then we have tried to discover the essential system of Islam, and to decide whether or not the Persian Shiah has been greatly influenced by the prophet's life and teaching. My own opinion is that Persia is most strongly Mohammedan, but seeing that the point of this book is not so much to express opinions as to give the facts that have led to their formation, I must not complain if many of my readers do not agree with me. An attempt has also been made to explain the religiosity of the Mohammedan, and to show that it is neither hypocrisy, nor yet religion in the Western sense. Then there was a chapter on the Yezdi's character, and I think that in this my main point was to show how superficial is the judgment that pronounces the Persian thoroughly weak and effete. He really shows great strength of purpose when he has a purpose, he has some peculiar abilities, and is at bottom thoroughly likeable and loveable, but he is spoilt by the unhappy circumstances of his existence and very specially by his creed.

After that there was an attempt to show the peculiar nature of the search after truth that is just now going on in Persia, and very particularly in Yezd. That this is God's doing, intended to prepare the way for Christian teaching, I have in my own mind no doubt at all; but I have tried to describe it as a phenomenon, and sometimes to trace it to immediate causes where such causes are easily discoverable. Lastly, I have tried to show that towns like Yezd present a field, not only workable by one class of missionary organisation, but approachable in many different ways.

I sincerely trust that those who have followed the argument of these chapters will have come to my own conclusion, that, although there are enormous difficulties in missionary work in Persia, there are also enormous opportunities, and that there is great reason to expect that in such a country things will one day come with a rush: further, that when the barrier of Mohammedanism is removed, there are grounds for hoping that Persian character will recover its equilibrium and the nation prove by no means decadent. If in addition the spiritual force of Christianity be brought to bear upon the people, Persia may prove in the future the missionary power of the near East. Persia at this moment is full of religious enquirers, willing to make immense sacrifices for their convictions; and behind these there is a mass of simple people, religiously minded and yet utterly dissatisfied with their present creed. There are of course great prejudices still existing against Christianity, but these prejudices have been by God's blessing broken down in individual instances, and when their nature is better realised they may more generally disappear. It is not necessary to give actual statistics with reference to converts: it is enough to say that the number of those who have come forward in Yezd is sufficient to prove two things; firstly, that God is willing to bless the work very fully, and secondly, that we are not quite ready for His blessing.[7]

If any further proof were needed of God's willingness to forward the work of the Yezd mission, it would be found in the history of the Christian institutions in the town. The medical work was founded by Dr Henry White about six years and a half back, he having been in the Isfahan district for about twelve months previous to his arrival in Yezd. There is now not only a men's hospital and dispensary in the town, but also two dispensaries in the outlying villages, and a women's hospital and dispensary under Dr Elsie Taylor. In connection with the medical work one can hardly help mentioning the name of Miss Bird, who really founded the work amongst the women, and that of Dr Griffith, who did most valuable work during the furlough of Dr White.

The site for the men's hospital was given to the Society shortly after Dr White's arrival, by the late Mr Gudarz, a prominent Parsi merchant in the town. The medical mission in Yezd may be said to be quite as firmly established as the Government.

I myself came to Yezd six months later than Dr White, without any previous experience of Persia. My successor, Mr Boyland, has now under his charge a school of about sixty boys, Mussulmans, Babis and Parsis, with a staff of native masters. The boys in spite of their religious differences play football together. The religious teaching in the school is given without the slightest concealment. There is also a school for Parsi girls more lately established by Miss Brighty. In this school religious instruction is also given. When I left Yezd the number of the pupils was about forty.

I may also mention that in the chapel which we have built in the hospital we often have congregations of over a hundred Persians. The chapel cost something under a hundred pounds, and the funds were subscribed, all but twenty-five pounds, by the members of the European colony.

It is a great mistake to regard such work as we have in Yezd as primarily of a preparatory nature in view of some future opportunity. Babiism, which is in some ways more opposed to Christianity than the religion of the average Persian Mussulman, is fast gaining ground, and the exceptional opportunity, which is occasioned by the preparation of the soil by Babi missionaries who have not yet been successful in planting their ideas, is fast passing away. It has been already pointed out that there is not much hope of real religious liberty under native rule.

Some people think that there are shortly going to be changes in Persia which will entirely deprive the British missionary of his opportunity. If we take this view we ought to act quickly. Taking a second and more hopeful view of the future, other political developments which might make religious liberty in any sense a reality, would find us by no means in a position to make the best use of them, unless we had a native church gathered in time of stress and strain upon whose judgment to rely.

Consequently mission work in Persia is a matter which demands most careful consideration, most unsparing effort, and most earnest prayer. We ought not to lack recruits. That there are difficulties to be solved is true, but when all has been said the overwhelming horror of modern Mohammedanism, the intense hopefulness of Persian character, and last but not least, the obvious preparation made by God in this country for human evangelistic labours, all together present a situation which cannot but appeal to the Christian Englishman.

FOOTNOTES

[1] The author has, with a few exceptions, accentuated native words *only* where they first occur in the book.

[3] The Yezdi realises the link of a common language, but by this he means a common dialect. Consequently I have included this idea in fellow-townsmanship; it in no way takes the place of the bond of country.

[4] I was informed, however, by Dr Griffith that the Mussulmans of Kirman welcomed his coming and the work of the medical mission on the ground that his *savabs*, being the *savabs* of an infidel, would be credited not to him but to the account of the Mohammedans of the town, who stood rather sorely in need of them.

[5] This only refers to visits of ceremony. When people found that they could come to my house without notice, I often had a continual succession of visitors throughout the day.

[6] Certainly the Light also operates inside Islam. During the Babi massacre a number of women who had been horrified by the sights in the streets said to my wife, "They say that we can't be Mussulmans if we mind these things, but cannot these things sicken even Mohammedans?"

[7] The opinion that Persia is changing its religion, or at least its form of Mohammedanism, is not confined to missionary circles.

GLOSSARY

Aivān	A kind of portico, or roofed recess.
Anjuman	Assembly, committee.
Arkhālūq	Under-coat.
Bābī	Follower of the Bāb.
Bād-gīr	Air-shaft.
Bāgh	Enclosed cultivation.
Behāī	Follower of Behāu'llah.
Chādar	Sheet; especially the cotton shawl worn over the head and whole body by the women.
Chārvādār	Muleteer, or donkey caravan driver.
Dastūr	Parsi priest.
Dīv	Demon.
Farrāsh	Literally a carpet-sweeper. Really a servant, chiefly outdoor.
Ferangī	Frank, European.
Firmān	Government order.
Islām	Resignation to God. The name given by Mohammed to his religion.
Jazīya	Poll tax levied by Mohammedans on non-Mohammedan monotheists living in their country.
Jin	Genius; a being composed of fire.
Kajāva	A kind of wooden pannier with a hood.
Khān	A hereditary title.
Krān	A coin worth about 4½d., the tenth part of a tomān.
Kursī	Wooden stool. Especially one used over a pan of charcoal to support a quilt.
Lāla	A spring candlestick with a globe.
Lūtī	A rough; a bad character.

Man'	A weight varying in different towns. In Yezd it is about 13 lbs.
Manzil	Halting-place.
Mazra'	A piece of cultivated land.
Mirzā	Clerk, secretary.
Muballigh	A missionary. The word is generally used of the Behāī missionaries in Yezd.
Mujtahid	The highest class of the Mohammedan clergy.
Mullā	A word very like our term "clerk." It is generally used of the clergy, but it is sometimes a mere courtesy title, and sometimes means a man who can read.
Mussulmān, Muslim	A believer in Islam. One who is resigned to God.
Nakhl	A religious implement.
Nijāsat	Ceremonial uncleanness.
Paighambar	Message bearer, prophet.
Paighambarī	Prophethood.
Qaba	Outer coat.
Qalāntar	Head-man. The title is used in Yezd for the head-man of the Parsis.
Qaliān	Persian hookah.
Qan'āt	Underground water-channel.
Raiyat	Agriculturist, a tenant farmer who pays rent in kind. It also means a subject.
Rūza khānī	Religious recitation.
Saughāt	A traveller's present.
Savāb	Work of merit.
Seyid	A descendant of Mohammed.
Shiah	Nonconformist. However, there is a Shiah sect held orthodox in Persia.
Sunnat	Ancient traditions and Commentary on the Quran accepted by the Sunnis.
Sunnī	A member of the Mohammedan sect accepting the Sunnat, who are considered orthodox in Turkey, India, and Africa, as opposed to the Shiahs of Persia and elsewhere.

Taqdīr	Predestination.
Taqīya	Concealment of faith by denial in times of danger.
Tauhīd	Assertion of the Divine Unity.
Tomān	A sum of money, 10,000 dinars, equivalent to about 3s. 8d.
Yailāq	Summer quarters, generally a village in the hills.
Zardūshtī	Follower of Zardūsht or Zoroaster, the Parsi prophet.

INDEX

Abbās

Abu Jahl

Abu Tālib, Mohammed's uncle

Aīvan

Ali, Imam

Ali Mohammed (Bab)

Anjuman

Arbāb Jamshīd, a wealthy Parsi at Tehran

Arches

Arkhālūq

Armenian Christians

Aryan Parsis

Atmosphere, absence of moisture in

Bāb, gate of knowledge

— —, first book-bearer of the Behāīs, founder of the Babi sect

Babis, the

massacre of

martyrs

Bād-gīr

Bāgh

Bazaars

Behāīs, the

massacre of,

tenets of,

Behaū'llah, first book-bearer of the Behāīs

Bigotry, in Yezd

Bird, Miss

Boyland, Mr

Brighty, Miss

Browne, Professor E. G., translator of the *Tārīkhi Jadīd*

Bruce, Canon

Carpenters, of Yezd

Carpets

Caspian Sea

Chādar

Chairs

Church Missionary Intelligencer

Church Missionary Society

Cleanliness, of Yezdis

Converts, problem of

Crime, indifference to

Curtains

Deserts, salt and sandy

Dīnyār, *Qalāntar* of the Parsi Committee

Divorce

Dīvs

Doors

Etiquette and Manners, of the Yezdis

European colony, in Yezd

Evil Eye

Fanaticism, of Yezdis

Farrāsh

Fireplaces

Fittings of houses

Flower-beds

Forgiveness of sins, Mohammed's teaching on the

Furniture

Gardens

Griffith, Dr

Gudarz, Mr, a prominent Parsi merchant of Yezd

Gypsum

Hakim Khānum, lady doctor

Hanifs, reformers

Hasan, Imam

Heaven and Hell, Mussulman idea of

Hill villages

Hookahs, Persian

Houses, built for heat

Husain, Imam

Huts, mud

Ibn Ishāk, the biographer

Ibrāhīm Qalīl Khān

Imam Ali

—— Hasan

—— Husain

Imams, the

Industrial missions—a suggestion

Infidels, Persian attitude towards

Insularity, of Yezd

Isaiah, quoted

Isfahan

Isfahanis, and Yezdis

Isfandiār, a Parsi schoolmaster at Taft

Islām, doctrine of

has ruined Persia

Isolation, of Yezd

Jadīd, a convert from Parsiism

Jalālu'd Daula, the

Jazīya

Jews, in Yezd

Mohammed's dealings with

Jins

Julfa, a suburb of Isfahan

Jus Paternum, in Yezd

Ka'aba, a heathen temple of the Meccans

Kāshān

Khadīja, wife of Mohammed

Khalīfs, the

Khauf u jizā, fear of hell and expectation of heaven

Kirmān

Koelle, *Life of Mohammed*

Kūcha Biyuk, village

Kursī

Lāla

Lamps

Language, Persian

Lāristān

Lattices

Ledges

Looking-glasses

Lūtīs

Mahdi, or Mehdi, the last of the Imams

Mānukjī Limjī, Parsi representative in Tehran

Manzil

Marriages, Persian

Mazra'

Mecca

Medical Missions, in Yezd

Medina,

Mihraban, a Parsi

Miracle play, Muharram

Missionary in Persia, the, his difficulties

the problem of converts

his tasks and duties

philanthropic work

poor relief

school and medical work

Missions, Christian, tolerated in Yezd

industrial

Mohammed

his birth

his wife

head of the *Hanif* movement

his admiration of the Jews

Mohammedanism, Persian

aspects in Yezd of

Monogamy

Mountain streams

Muballigh, teacher and missionary

Mud, use of

huts of

Muhammad Hasan Khan, Governor of Yezd

Muharram

Mujtahid

Mulla Bahrām of Khuramshār, a Parsi

Munāfiqīn, hypocrites

Mushīru'l Mamālik, the

Mussulman *v.* Armenian morality

Muzaffaru'd Dīn, Shah

Nakhl

Nāsiru'd Dīn, Shah

Nāsiru'd Dīn, Mulla, and his mule, story of

Nijāsat

Non-conformity in Persia

Oasis

Omar, Khalīf

Opium trade

Ornamentation, of houses

Paighambarī

Parsis in Yezd, oppression and persecution of

Pilgrimages, Mussulman

Plain, a typical Persian

Polygamy

Poor relief

Postal arrangements, in Yezd

Qabā

Qalāntar

Qaliān

Qum

Qurān, the

Rainfall

Ramazān, Mohammedan Fast

Rasht

Rice, Rev. W. A.

Rustami Ardishīri Dīnyār, a Parsi

Rūza khānī

Sahāmu'l Mulk

Sāhibi kitāb, a book-bearer, Mohammed regarded as the last

Salāmat, a Parsi

Salt and sandy deserts

Saughāts

Savābs

School work, in Yezd

Seyid, a descendant of Mohammed

Shaikhi sect, the

Shahr, a town

Shiahs, or nonconformists

Shīrāz

Silkworms

Soldiers, Persian

Streams, mountain

Subhi Azal, second book-bearer of the Behāīs

Sufis, sect of the

Summer buildings

Sunnat

Sunnis, and their creed

Superstition

Tables

Taft village

Tālār, summer portico

Tāqchas, ledges

Taqdīr

Taqiya

Tārīkhi Jadīd

Tauhid

Taylor, Dr Elsie

Teheran

Telegraph line, native

Tīrandāz, a Parsi

Toman

Trinket boxes

Turners, of Yezd

Uncleanness, degrees of

Untruthfulness of Persians

Vatan, home-district

Villages

hill

Walls, house

Waraka ibn Nawfal, a prominent *Hanif*

Water system

White, Dr Henry

Windows

Winter rooms

Yailāq

Yazīd

Yezd district, houses in

its isolation and insularity

Yezdis, and Isfahanis
their religion
character of the
systematised inconsistency
loyalty
sense of shame
humour
their disregard of time
difficulties of their language
lack of initiative
their courage
etiquette and manners of
their triviality
pride
kindliness, cruelty
dishonesty
lack of business habits
fatalism
latent strength
their family ties
jus paternum
religious liberty
indifference to crime
open-handness
Zaid
Zaid ibn Amr
Zainab
Zardūshtī (Zoroastrian)
Zillu's Sultān
Zoroastrians, in Yezd